THEY'RE H
LAST YOU
OUT ABOUT

—The devastatingly logical reason why in ancient times aliens from outer space landed in certain areas, while ignoring others.

—The hidden code found in the Bible and other sacred writings.

—Plants that have been affected by the presence of aliens and what we can learn from their reaction.

—Actual messages that have been received from the aliens.

—New cases of abductions and forced sexual activity by extraterrestrials.

—The shocking new evidence that aliens may be ready to take over the earth!

READ THIS BOOK IF YOU DARE FACE THE TRUTH!

THE ALIEN AGENDA

THE
ALIEN
AGENDA

by

Dr. Clifford Wilson, Ph.D.

(The updated and expanded edition of *UFOs . . . and Their Mission Impossible*)

A SIGNET BOOK

NEW AMERICAN LIBRARY

A DIVISION OF PENGUIN BOOKS USA INC.

SIGNET TRADEMARK REG. U.S. PAT. OFF. AND FOREIGN COUNTRIES
REGISTERED TRADEMARK—MARCA REGISTRADA
HECHO EN DRESDEN, TN, U.S.A.

SIGNET, SIGNET CLASSIC, MENTOR, ONYX, PLUME, MERIDIAN
and NAL BOOKS are published by New American Library, a division of
Penguin Books USA Inc., 1633 Broadway, New York, New York 10019

First Revised Edition Printing, September, 1988
First Printing, April, 1975

6   7   8   9   10   11   12   13   14

PRINTED IN THE UNITED STATES OF AMERICA

Contents

Preface vii

1: The UFOs Are Here 1

2: The Credibility of the Witnesses 10

3: Contact Is Made 22

4: UFOs—USA or USSR? 32

5: Incredible Contact Tales 41

6. Friendly or Hostile? 52

7: Sightings Through the Centuries:
   And the Chariots Still Crash 66

8: Hoaxes and Hallucinations 86

9: On Mushrooms, Mirages and Myopia:
   But Who Did Have Myopia? 98

10: A Hollow Earth? A Parallel World?
    Another Planet? 116

11: Electromagnetic Power?
    An Antigravitational Force? 134

12: The Paraphysical Explanation 149

13: Vampires and UFOs 168

14: The Bible and UFOs 186

15: A Personal Note 210

16: An Update: The Alien Agenda Progresses . . .216

    Notes 228

    Bibliography 234

Preface

Some time ago I was asked if I would make a series of radio talks in answer to Erich Von Daniken's best-sellers, *Chariots of the Gods?* and *Return to the Stars.* At the time the subject did not especially interest me, and I declined. Various friends persisted, however, and in the end I agreed to make a series of radio talks, and from these grew the manuscript that became a best-selling book, *Crash Go the Chariots.* Since then I have appeared at many public meetings, and have taken part in a great number of talk-back shows on both radio and television. The questions hurled at me have gone way beyond the material contained in *Crash Go the Chariots,* as have the letters which have come to me from many parts of the world. Perhaps I am naïve to admit it, but I have been amazed at the tremendous interest there is in the subject of "flying saucers," the occult, and the Bible.

Many times I have been asked, "Do you personally believe in UFOs?" and my answer has usually been, "I certainly do not disbelieve in them." I suppose my own experience is similar to that of many others: ten years ago I would have regarded belief in UFOs as unthink-able—the sort of thing that should be confined to people who are always looking for way-out theories and beliefs. Then several years ago I watched a television news coverage in my own home city of Melbourne, Australia. Many people had reported seeing a UFO, and a number of schoolboys were separately asked to draw what they had seen. There were variations, but it was obvious that either these boys were deliberately concocting a story with the help of the TV interviewer, or they really had seen something that was beyond explanation in known terms.

As I watched, I was surprised to find that I was satis-fied that these boys really had seen something. Their drawings were by no means all exactly the same, but the configurations were sufficiently close to indicate they were describing the same thing.

I was satisfied with the sincerity of those boys. That of course is not proof that there were UFOs, but to me it was a new stage. It was interesting to contrast my reactions to those I had experienced several years earlier in Wellington, New Zealand. One of the largest newspapers in that dominion came out with a whole series of pictures of flying saucers and although they seemed convincing photographically, somehow there was a reservation. Sure enough, a day or two later the newspaper itself came out with a full explanation of the way in which the various "saucers" had been photographed. One was the splash from a blob of milk, photographed with fast film just after the blob bounced back from the floor. Others had similar explanations.

Because of fakes such as this—and many such fakes have been perpetrated—the less credulous people across the world have been slow to accept that UFOs should be taken seriously. Indeed, one's reputation was likely to be lessened if he acknowledged the possibility of UFOs being real, but now all that is changed. Sightings have taken place in the thousands, with large numbers of people reporting them at specific points of time and location.

Are they a mass delusion? Can they all be explained as "natural phenomena"? In this volume the attempt has been made to lay aside prejudices and preconceived notions. Indeed, the book that has developed is considerably more elaborate and touches on more areas than was at first intended. The original draft had to be completely rewritten, for it became obvious that the subject involved much more than I expected when I began researching.

I soon found that UFO writers did not fit into a mold, for some were diametrically opposed to others in their approach. There are science fiction writers for whom this exciting new realm is fair game; there are Bible students and scholars who enthusiastically believe in UFO activity at various points in the Bible; there are those who dogmatically assert that we are being invaded by beings from other planets; just as emphatic are some who proclaim that angelic beings are standing by to rescue an army of earthlings at a soon-coming time when earth itself will be destroyed by man's own folly.

A number of writers cannot be taken seriously, for a variety of reasons. Undoubtedly there are hoaxes and hallucinations, prejudices and perversions, distortions and deceptions—and one is inclined to throw out the baby with the proverbial bath water.

Another theory is that UFO occupants are hostile scouts from another planet, preparing for a soon-coming invasion, while other writers, who are more earthbound, are sure that the first UFO to be thoroughly examined will carry the sign "Made in Russia." Some even insist that they really are experimental craft, hushed up, the information withheld, but really being secret United States spacecraft.

If, then, the UFOs are real, how long have they been here? What evidence is there of sightings through the centuries? What about the weird stories of falling stones and rocks (and even potato peelings!)?

These stories seem well-nigh incredible. So also do those about "spacenappings" of children, adults, animals, and possibly even airplanes. Therefore, how credible are the witnesses—crackpots, or do they include highly acceptable persons, people whose testimony would be accepted in a court of law? Contrary to the opinions of many, the answer is in the affirmative, as we will proceed to show in this volume.

Accepting the credibility of the witnesses and the fact of UFOs, what then? Are they extraterrestrial vehicles utilizing an anti-gravitational force? And what part does electromagnetism play?

Or are they "paraphysical" objects and beings in the same category as demons and spirits, séances and other manifestations of the occult?

What about the Bible—are there UFOs in the Bible? If not, how about the crossing of the Red Sea, Ezekiel's vision, Elijah in a chariot of horses and fire, the Star of Bethlehem?

There have been many reports of messages from UFOs—how authentic are they? Has radio contact been made? How do the messages compare with those coming from other nonearthly sources?

The questions are fascinating, and they are highly relevant today. We even find a new "scientific respectability" given to the possibility of earth being originally populated by space beings. Is it myth, legend, fact, or devilish delusion? How do we explain such a change in the attitude of some men of science?

And now, over a decade has passed since this book first appeared. The same questions are still being asked and the stories we tell you in the following pages have stood the test of investigation.

But it does not stop there. There have been dramatic new developments, especially with the release of thousands of pages of classified information under the Freedom of Information Act. And it is that material and more which makes possible this new edition.

THE
ALIEN
AGENDA

Chapter 1

The UFOs Are Here

The days of doubt have ended. The fact is—whether we like it or not—the UFOs are here. They have landed in the USA and Australia, in England and France, in Russia and Mexico, at both the North and the South Poles.

Cigar-shaped as well as disk-like; some are hundreds of feet across and others only a few inches; some with occupants and some without; at times seeming to be friendly but at other times spacenapping a father, a child, a horse, or a dog—and their activity is increasing, not lessening.

Twenty years ago anyone claiming to believe in flying saucers was looked at with an amused smile—but not any more. Despite the fact that saucer sightings are no longer international news, so many reputable witnesses have seen them that the world has had to listen—and to believe, even though that belief is still expressed only in a soft whisper.

What has brought about the change? And what is the answer to the UFO phenomenon? We shall consider some of the facts, then examine the main theories—even if they are frightening. Maybe then we will have a better idea as to what the most likely answer is.

Undoubtedly there have been many genuine sightings before 1947 and we shall consider a number of these. However, in that year the modern furor about saucers was set off by a private pilot from Idaho named Kenneth Arnold. On June 24 he was flying near Mount Rainier, Washington, when he sighted nine gleaming disks racing along at an estimated speed of more than 1,000 miles an hour, and about 100 feet in diameter.

He described them as being saucerlike, and the name flying saucers was born. This very name tended to give the whole concept an air of fantasy, and they were ridiculed from the start. Serious investigation had to overcome this unfortunate beginning.

Within a few days of Kenneth Arnold's sighting there were reports of many sightings all over the United States, and of course there were the inevitable hoaxes. Because of the great rash of reports many believed this was a case of mass hysteria, and it is probable that it was a legitimate explanation for many so-called sightings. However, it was not all the answer. Hard-headed skeptics such as civilian airlines' ground crews and pilots reported disks at various bases, and this was true of U.S. Air Force pilots as well.

Right from the beginning, official statements were contradictory—one highly reputable authority, Major Donald Keyhoe, gives an example of an official statement that the saucers were only hallucinations while on the same day air force officers at Dayton openly admitted that the Air Materiel Command was, in fact, seriously investigating the phenomenon.[1]

Should the Reports Be Taken Seriously?

There have been many reports of UFOs—of controlled flying objects—before airplanes were known in modern times. From the end of World War II there have been an increasing number of reports, but these were not taken very seriously for a number of years. Even the famous sighting by the Anglican priest, Reverend William Gill, in New Guinea in 1959, was taken by many with a grain of salt—and that despite the fact that thirty-seven witnesses testified to the events he described. A spacecraft was seen a short distance from them, figures emerged and reentered the vehicle over a period of hours, waved back when Reverend Gill waved to them, and eventually took off again.[2]

The reports have persisted, in countries as far apart as the United States and New Zealand and Australia, and even a reputedly skeptical land such as France reported many sightings in the 1950s. Nevertheless, most people refused to believe in these things, partly because of the associated sensationalism, and partly because of some not-to-be-taken-seriously firsthand reports of men who had traveled to far-flung planets in the company of beautiful maidens. In addition, the whole idea of spacecraft and of extraterrestrial beings was somehow quite unacceptable. It tended to detract from our dignity as unique dwellers, alone in the universe.

As time went by, and sightings were no longer a rarity, the subject tended to pass out of public interest. In addition, it was established that undoubtedly many reports of flying saucers were not of flying saucers at all. Planets—especially Venus, cloud formations, weather and other balloons, searchlights, fast-flying aircraft, "falling stars," satellites, atmospheric conditions, mental delusions, and straight-out deceptions and hoaxes—all these played their part. Other explanations centered around practical jokes, optical illusions, mirages, collective hallucinations, and even birds. Then, too, sometimes journalists were guilty of unfortunate sensationalism, with deliberate gross exaggerations and distortions of many so-called sightings.

Another factor which helped to lessen public interest was the nonsympathetic attitude of some sections of the press. For many years any mention of flying saucers was in the "funny file." However, there are illustrations throughout history that what is in the "funny file" today may be looked on as serious business tomorrow. Some years ago Immanuel Velikovsky dared to put out a number of arguments and hypotheses which opposed "established" scientific theories. He was criticized, and his scholarship was challenged, yet today it is recognized that some things—not all by any means—he had to say should be taken seriously after all. Perhaps something similar has happened with the world's press in relation to flying saucers. The press no longer reports UFOs with a sneer, but tends to regard them as serious factual matter.

However, the evidence goes beyond press reports. One of the best investigative reports in the early 1950s was entitled "The Report on Unidentified Flying Objects" by Edward J. Ruppelt.[3] Ruppelt was a captain in the Air Force, and headed "Project Blue Book" which the United States government set up in an attempt to solve the UFO mystery. Ruppelt examined thousands of reports or records of supposed sightings and retained only those he felt had reasonable claims to genuineness. The American reports recognized a sighting as genuine only when no "natural" explanation could be put forward. In addition, the object supposedly sighted had to be observed by witnesses on the ground, by pilots of military aircraft actually flying at the time, and on radar screens. According to Paul Thomas,[4] sightings that conformed to these three conditions were put in a file marked "Unexplained." At that time the possibility of intrusion from another planet was not considered an acceptable explanation for official purposes.

According to "Project Blue Book," between 1947 and 1962 a fraction under 2 percent of the sightings in the United States could not be explained, this being in the United States alone.[5] In addition, very many of the official explanations were unconvincing even to those who gave them. The evidence has convinced representatives of many walks of life—varying social classes and religious groups, people of high intelligence, and others not so endowed. The eminent psychologist, Carl G. Jung of Zurich, is one who wrote that it cannot be doubted that the flying saucers that have appeared on radar screens and occasional photographic plates are actually genuine.[6]

Another who helped cause a revolution in thinking was the French writer, M. Aimé Michel.[7] In his book *Mysterieux Objets Celestes* he showed that the French sightings on particular days were exactly in straight lines that stretched across some 600 miles in length. A recent series of sightings in Australia was rather similar—stretching across the northwest area of Australia from the Indian Ocean to Central Australia and back again, being reported by a large number of reliable witnesses. The objective evidence put forward by M. Michel made it clear that this was not some collective hallucination or coincidence. It led to the reputable magazine *Science and Life* (*Science et Vie*) breaking its previously rigid silence on UFOs and, in February, 1958, it highlighted Michel's findings, and published a map which made clear the importance of his discovery. In the years that have followed, Michel's straight-line theory has been modified, but his basic pattern of sightings is still accepted.

Tracked on Radar

We stress that whatever these things are, they have been tracked on radar many times. A typical evidence of that comes from Lieutenant-Colonel Herbert Rolph of the North American Air Defense Command Center at Colorado Springs in Colorado. The colonel admitted to a gathering of newspaper reporters that on Wednesday April 18, 1962, his Defense Center had tracked an object on radar right across the United States.[8] Many similar trackings have been made.

As one reads extensively through the literature dealing with sightings, it becomes clear that there are a great number of different shapes associated with these unidentified flying objects. Brinsley Le Poer Trench lists 63 distinct shapes, and suggests that other types will also be recognized as the record of sighting becomes more complete.[9]

There are UFOs in the shapes of disks, triangles, spheres, cigars, UFOs with wings and with wheels, some with flat domes and others having no domes at all. They are reported in all colors of the spectrum. There are even some reported as unmarked airplanes or unidentified helicopters, and reports of various shapes and sizes keep coming in from many parts of the world.[10]

There have been small disklike objects capable of

fantastic acceleration and speed, often sighted in groups flying in formation. Others are described as like rockets, or as cosmic ray balloon types, with variations in the words used, but stressing fantastic speeds beyond anything made by man. A common terminology is that the main body of the saucer looked like a large cigar, especially when this was used to describe a mother ship from which numerous smaller disks would fly out and later return.

We have shown in passing that these sightings are not limited to the United States of America. On July 19, 1962, the whole body of 150 workmen at the Auto Union D.K.W. Car Plant, at Sauce Viejo, northwest of Buenos Aires, watched a cigar-shaped UFO moving toward the northeast. It seemed to be only about 100 meters in the air, and was giving out blinding flashes. It left no trail behind, and soon it climbed rapidly and disappeared. Some of the observers had seen the same type of craft a number of times previously over the same area.[11]

Brinsley Le Poer Trench gives a whole series of sightings associated with South America, with dates and names of highly reputable witnesses.[12] He then draws conclusions as to the possibilities of UFOs establishing bases in the sparsely populated areas of that subcontinent. It would seem, however, that the evidence for this conclusion is not altogether convincing, for the mere fact of so many sightings seems to suggest that, if we accept them as real, part of the idea is to be seen— these vehicles are certainly not restricted to sparsely populated areas.

Sightings in Australia

In this author's own country of Australia there have been many seemingly reputable reports of sightings— including one report by three separate witnesses as this chapter is being edited! When one hears from personal pilot friends that they are briefed concerning the areas where UFOs are seen most frequently, it becomes obvious that authorities are no longer unconvinced as to the fact of so-called flying saucers.

When some of those personal friends hesitate to tell of what they have seen because of their fear of ridicule, and then it turns out that their stories are similar to those told over the world, one would be burying his head in the sand to insist, "There is no such thing!"

The attitude toward flying saucers has changed in Australia. The January 11, 1967, edition of *Everybody's*, a countrywide magazine, included a large map of Australia listing 70 spots where saucers had been sighted. Alongside was a brief caption such as, "No. 62 - Long Reach, Queensland, July 23, 1964, Reverend I. W. Alcorn. 10 delta-shaped objects, circled at 50,000 feet for three minutes." As the brief descriptions are read, telling of objects that accelerated at great speed, while other reports speak of green, red, and white lights—or yet again of objects that hover over limited areas and then flash off into the sky—the pattern is clearly similar to that which is reported in so many other parts of the world.

These reports are not from "mental cases," or from people anxious to see saucers. This is illustrated by one of the most interesting reports in Australia, of "flying saucer nests" reported to have been found in the Tully district in Queensland. There were circular clearings of dry reeds, surrounded by green reeds that were unaffected. One of those who sighted this "nest" was a twenty-seven-year-old banana grower named George Pedley, who reported seeing a vaporlike saucer take off from one of these nests.

"Had anyone asked me five days ago if I believed in flying saucers I'd have laughed and thought they were nuts," he said. "But now I know better. I've actually seen a spaceship. No one will ever convince me that I was imagining things. I was driving the tractor through a neighboring property on my way to my farm about 9 A.M. on Wednesday when I heard a loud hissing noise above the engine noise of the tractor. It sounded like air escaping from a tire. But the tractor tires seemed okay, so I drove on. At first I ignored the sound, but suddenly I saw a spaceship rise at great speed out of a swamp called Horse Shoe Lagoon about 25 yards in front of me. It was blue-gray, about 25 feet across and 9 feet high. It spun at a terrific rate as it rose vertically to about 60 feet, and then made a shallow dive and rose sharply. Traveling at a fantastic speed, it headed off in a southwesterly direction. It was out of sight in seconds. I saw no portholes or antennae," Mr. Pedley said, "and there was no sign of life either in or about the ship."[13]

The report goes on to state that dozens of cases of flying saucers have been reported in the Tully area during the previous two months. Other people also told their stories, with remarkable similarities to other sightings referred to throughout this book.

It is interesting to observe that about one third of the sightings of spacecraft have been over bodies of water. Some UFO researchers have suggested that there is a UFO base on the moon which has no water, and so water is being siphoned up for use on their camp located on the moon—an explanation, by the way, which this author does not accept!

However, the report of taking water, and of searching for something in the sea, is referred to very often. If the paraphysical explanation for UFOs is accepted,[14] it might be that elements found in the oceans have very real significance for the temporary "solid" phenomena involved in these sightings.

Sometimes these incidents are out at sea, and are similar to those where aircraft were supposed to be paced. One such report is in the log of HMS *Vulture*, under Commander Pringle when cruising in the Persian Gulf on May 15, 1879.[15] He wrote that two incredible objects, glowing brightly, were pacing his ship, one on each side. He described them as being like a revolving wheel with illuminated spokes, and that the one on the west side of the ship seemed to be revolving in the opposite direction to the one on the east side.

There are also many modern reports of spacecraft

zooming straight out of the sea and away into the sky. Hardline ufologists suggest that beings in these craft are examining sea life in the same way they are examining animal life and even human life. Others insist that this activity is associated with military bases of some sort—in these cases, underwater bases where they would be relatively safe from investigation or attack.

We have stressed in other parts of this volume that the reports have been persistent long before the recent rash of so-called sightings. We shall examine some of these in our chapter "UFOs Through the Ages."

It is often suggested that these vehicles are merely demonstrating technological achievements whose secret is as yet unknown to the man in the street. However, we shall see that no national power on the planet earth has achieved such a breakthrough. Our point at the moment is that, whether we accept the UFO phenomena as being explained by beings utilizing electromagnetism, or insist that the answer lies in the paraphysical realm, UFOs are with us. They will not go away, though they might very well be reported less and less in our newspapers. After all, none of us runs outside to see an airplane anymore, as this writer did when he was a little boy!

Many years have passed since this book was first published. It has become increasingly clear in time that UFOs are not mere figments of the imagination. Today, even more than when the following stories were originally written, their critics are not so vocal. The release of formerly secret records has suddenly caused skeptics to look the other way.

Read on. These stories are not farcical. They are no longer explainable as crackpot lies and hoaxes, and this writer knows of countless people around the world who can tell of similar incidents. That similarity is itself an indicator of their genuineness.

So read on, and discover that the witnesses *are* credible.

Chapter 2

The Credibility of
the Witnesses

Courts of law are slow to accept damaging testimony from witnesses whose credibility has been rejected. To discredit the witness is a legal tactic, and there is clear evidence that efforts have at times been made to debunk the evidence of "saucer" sightings by discrediting the witnesses.

An excellent "confession" to this effect comes from Dr. J. Allen Hynek, chairman of the Department of Astronomy at Northwestern University at Evanston in Illinois. He was the top astronomer officially involved with the U.S. "Project Sign" for the investigation of possible astronomical phenomena involved with UFOs. Dr. Hynek's book *The UFO Experience: A Scientific Inquiry*, is partly the story of his own journey from amused skepticism to scientific acknowledgment of the "reality" of UFOs.

At one point Dr. Hynek tells of his investigation of a supposed sighting of UFO occupants by Lonnie Zamora, a policeman in Socorro, New Mexico, on April 24, 1964. He writes:[1]

> My original investigation, directed toward breaking apart Zamora's account by seeking mutual contradictions in it and also by seeking to establish Zamora as an unreliable witness, was fruitless. I was impressed by the high regard in which Zamora was held by his colleagues, and I personally am willing today to accept his testimony as genuine, particularly since it does fit a global pattern.

10

". . . seeking mutual contradictions . . . seeking to establish Zamora as an unreliable witness . . ." These are not the statements of a disreputable person but of a man of great integrity—a first-class scientist committed to an honest appraisal, and that honest appraisal has led to the publication of this outstanding report on his own investigations. Clearly he himself became convinced as to the credibility of many—though not all—witnesses, and the facts demand acceptance.

Vehement "Official" Denials

Sometimes the official denials have been vehement, as when Colonel Harold E. Watson, chief of intelligence for AMC in the United States, told interviewer Bob Considine that there were no such things as flying saucers and went on to brand most saucer witnesses as practical jokers, crackpots, religious cranks, or publicity hounds.[2] He admitted that some who reported seeing them might be honest, and he included in that category airline pilots who mistook windshield reflections for spaceships when they themselves were suffering from fatigue. This sort of official denouncement has caused many pilots to be extremely wary of reporting saucer sightings, or of making relevant entries in their flight logs.

At other times the official denials have been of a different type. An example is the denial as to the factuality of what Frank Scully reported in his book *Behind the Flying Saucers*—that two flying disks from Venus had crashed in the United States and that the investigators had found the bodies of several little men in this vehicle. According to Scully, the U.S. Air Force had spirited both the bodies and the vehicle away for secret analysis. Although Scully insisted that the sources for this information were credible, his story could not be substantiated.

This does not imply that all U.S. defense personnel have remained "anti-saucer." Obviously Edward J. Ruppelt must be considered a reliable witness. We have

already referred to him as the head of "Project Blue
Book," and in his official capacity he did much to sub-
due the fears of the public, especially in times of saucer
flaps. However, over a period the evidence greatly impressed Captain Ruppelt. Donald Keyhoe quotes him
as saying:[3]

> What constitutes proof? Does a UFO have to land at
> the river entrance to the Pentagon, near the joint
> chiefs-of-staff offices? Or is it proof when a ground ra-
> dar station detects a UFO, sends a jet to intercept it,
> the jet pilot sees it, and locks on with his radar, only to
> have the UFO streak away at a phenomenal speed? Is it
> proof when a jet pilot fires at a UFO and sticks to his
> story even under the threat of court-martial? Does this
> constitute proof?

In retrospect it seems incredible that a court-martial
could be threatened for such an "offense." It almost
smacks of the darkness we sometimes associate with the
Middle Ages. Yet the fact is that only slowly has
"modern" man of this generation come to accept the reality of these strange visitors in their incredible space
vehicles.

Keyhoe gives an excellent summary of the personnel
included in reports on UFOs.[4] Besides the air force,
navy, and marine corps sightings, this file included reports by general military personnel—radar men, guided
missile trackers, crews of naval vessels, and members of
ground combat forces. In addition, there have been
sightings by especially competent civilians such as aeronautical engineers, airport traffic controllers, weather
bureau observers, astronomers, ground observer corps
members, FBI agents, state, county and city police,
reputable private pilots, and others who should certainly
be regarded as competent observers. The group included
veteran airliner crews—captains and co-pilots of American, United, Eastern, Pan-American, North West, Chi-
gago and Southern, Mid-Continent, Western, Trans-
World, and many other lines.

Paul Thomas refers to the "merciless pruning"[5] of
sightings—and gives thought-provoking evidence to

suggest that officials have all too often had a blind spot to the possibility of an actual phenomenon in the skies around the world. Very many of the witnesses have been utterly reputable, and their credibility would not have been challenged in a less sensational area. To an unprejudiced investigator, it would have been hard to find a group better qualified to observe and report on the UFOs. Nevertheless the remarkable fact is that since 1947 these men have been publicly ridiculed time and time again.

First-Class Witnesses

Keyhoe himself talked to many who claimed to have seen saucers—"rocket designers, aircraft engineers, flight surgeons and Washington officers I knew personally from my days at Annapolis. Among the latter were Captain (now Admiral) Delmir Fahrney, who was then top figure in the navy guided missile program, and Admiral Calvin Bolster, another Naval Academy classmate of mine."[6] At the time Admiral Bolster was in charge of the special design section of the Bureau of Aeronautics. He was emphatic to Keyhoe that he himself was puzzled by the sightings, and that he was in a position to know that the answer did not relate to anything that the United States was doing.

The U.S. Air Force clearly recognized Major Keyhoe as an utterly reliable witness. In an appendix to that same book from which the above quote is taken, he encloses an official list of Air Technical Intelligence UFO sightings, and other information secured and cleared for him by Mr. Albert M. Chop of tht U.S. Air Force press desk.[7] In the 1950s Donald Keyhoe was accredited by the U.S. Air Force as relatively few other journalists have been accredited. He himself had been a major in the U.S. Air Force, and his writings have been taken seriously by scientists, United States government personnel, and ufologists—which is a new term denoting those who study UFOs. There were times when

Keyhoe was the only civilian allowed to be present at important conferences involving defense personnel.

It is not our intention simply to make this book a report or a formal list of UFO sightings, contacts, etc., but as one reads Keyhoe's *Flying Saucers from Outer Space* it becomes impossible not to accept the fact that there is a phenomenon in our midst that must be taken seriously. Those who regard this merely as a subject to be scoffed at, looking on all those who have seen flying saucers as being in need of psychiatric help, should read Keyhoe's book. The unbiased reader will at least put it down with the conclusion that the subject cannot be dismissed lightly.

Many others besides defense personnel have come to believe in this "new" phenomenon. UFO literature often lists names of highly reputable and/or famous persons who have declared themselves as believing in the possibility of such concepts as attacks from other planets. A typical example is *The Australian Flying Saucer Review* of November, 1962, in which George A. Tararin quotes Canada's former Foreign Minister, Lester B. Pearson, the then Soviet Deputy Premier Kozlov, the late General Douglas MacArthur, Malcolm Muggeridge, and the late former President Dwight Eisenhower as all recognizing that there is something that should be seriously considered.

Thor Heyerdahl

Thor Heyerdahl is well known for his Kon-Tiki expedition, and for his other investigations and voyages. He journeyed across the Atlantic in his papyrus boat *Ra II* and logged three strange sightings—one in the early hours of June 10, 1970, when he himself saw a bright orange light which he was sure was not the light of a ship; the following night two crew members saw an orange flame slowly moving across the sky, and then three weeks later, on June 30, the man on watch, together with Thor Heyerdahl himself and two other crewmen, watched a light that was dome-shaped, and actually grew in size as they watched. One of the witnesses described it as being many times brighter than the moon, casting an illuminated path across the water, and silhouetting two small clouds that drifted between it and the papyrus boat. Then it spread along the horizon as though it was a giant mushroom cloud, finally losing its distinct shape and becoming more diffuse.[8]

As with some of the other sightings, it could be argued that this third phenomenon was some sort of atmospheric testing device, but the first two are hard to explain by the glib use of words such as "natural phenomena."

Many of the sightings have been in the presence of great numbers of people, such as that over the city of Indianapolis on July 13, 1952.[9] A huge oval-shaped machine was seen racing over the city, barely 5,000 feet above the ground. It was witnessed by thousands of people, and almost immediately the switchboards of the police, the newspaper offices, and the airport were swamped with citizens—many of them frightened—either asking for information or reporting the facts. Just before the actual sighting, air force radar had picked up a high-flying craft in the area.

The witnesses were not all on the ground, for a number of airline pilots also saw this strange vehicle. Pilots from American Air Lines, Eastern Air Lines, and another from the U.S. Air Force were among those who soberly told of this UFO with the fantastic speed. Previously some of these had been outright skeptics, but were now convinced of the reality of these strange vehicles.

There was a measure of public hysteria and near-panic, but the saucer did not return and the situation fairly quickly returned to normal. Official reticence at acknowledging the reality of flying saucers was seen to have some basis of wisdom, for the public reaction to this close sighting by thousands of people had made it clear that if a large saucer were to land there could well be a stampede on a mammoth scale.

With individual sightings, one argument often used

to suggest that the witnesses were not reliable was that over and over again the descriptions of the vehicles were not exactly the same. However, others point out that if there was an attempt at collusion then the descriptions would be made to fit, and this obviously has not happened. In any case, we earthlings have a vast number of different types of motor cars and even aircraft, and surely the same would be expected of vehicles produced by superintelligent beings, whether from outer space or elsewhere. On the other hand, the similarities are such that there must be at least a shred of truth behind the great mass of sightings, not only by individuals but also by large numbers of people simultaneously.

Photographs of UFOs and Newspaper Reports

Even photographs of UFOs have been issued in recent years. The first in modern times seems to have been taken on August 12, 1883, by a Mexican astronomer, José Bonilla.[10] From his observatory at Zacatecas he suddenly saw a whole parade of 143 circular objects which flitted across the disk of the sun. His telescope was equipped with that new invention, the camera, and he actually took pictures of these strange phenomena. When his film was developed, he had a series of cigar- and spindle-shaped objects which were "solid" and noncelestial.

There are many other reports, including photographs, which demand to be taken seriously. *Life International* of April 18, 1966, has a series of colored photographs and a report headed "A Well-Witnessed 'Invasion' by Something." It describes how from Australia to Michigan there has been a flurry of eerie UFO sightings. Once again, the reports were written by serious investigators, presenting evidence consistent with much that has come from many places. It is relevant to comment that there have been many genuine photographs taken, even from as remote a place as Antarctica.[11]

Not all investigators have accepted the "visitors from space" theory: later in this book we discuss some of the implications of *The Condon Report*, an official U.S. report on the UFO phenomenon, published in January, 1969. That report basically suggested that UFOs can be explained only in paraphysical terms, as with spiritual phenomena. That does not preclude the "solid" reality—at least temporarily solid—of UFOs, and reports of sightings continue to be made on a worldwide basis.

One of the most interesting books on the UFO phenomenon since the issue of *The Condon Report* was John A. Keel's *UFOs—Operation Trojan Horse*. Just as Donald Keyhoe's *Flying Saucers from Outer Space* spoke with authority based on the information available in the early 1950s, in a somewhat similar way John Keel speaks with authority in the early 1970s. He does not dwell on actual sightings as such, nor on side issues as to the importance or otherwise of government policy, nor on discussions of personalities and "contactees."

As he presents his case, the basic credibility of the witnesses becomes even more clearly established, for the number of sightings has not lessened since the publication of *The Condon Report* in 1969. John Keel himself had decided to investigate the matter of UFOs more seriously in March, 1966, and part of his research involved subscribing to newspaper clipping services. He was amazed to find that sometimes he would receive as many as 150 clippings for one day.[12] His initial reaction was one of disbelief, thinking that newspapers across the United States had put objectivity to one side and were involved in sensationalism. However, he soon changed his mind. In hundreds of interviews he found that a great number of the witnesses were reasonable men, with good standing in the community.

As he investigated the newspaper reports he usually found that the editors and journalists were themselves publishing well-validated stories, and not simply engaging in some sort of "gigantic put-on." In the main the newspapers had a policy of concentrating on sightings reported by local officers or officials. Keel found that literally thousands of sightings were being reported by less prominent citizens to newspapers, but their stories were not being published. Even though hundreds of stories were being reported each day, it became clear that these represented only a fraction of the whole.

Keel traveled many thousands of miles, going through twenty states of the United States of America, interviewing thousands of people. At times he found himself dealing with liars and publicity-seekers, but in the main those who claimed to have sighted saucers were ordinary and honest human beings. Very often he found they would not discuss their story until he had reassured them and had gained their confidence—many feared they would be ridiculed or even slandered. It was obvious they did not know that many other people had had similar experiences, but, as the details were related to Keel, they corroborated many similar experiences. Keel himself insists that he maintained secrecy as to other sightings, and "by maintaining this secrecy, I was able to make unique correlations that might not otherwise have been possible."[13]

It is true that a number of ufologists have overinterpreted their material and have added coloring that suited their own particular point of view. John Keel discusses this, and then makes the observation that some UFO organizations even had the tendency to delete reported details if they felt those details would detract from their own point of view. Unfortunately many people think this is true of all UFO writings, but this is not the case. This writer for one has been agreeably surprised at the objectivity of much that has been reported in UFO journals and books, though this is not meant as an endorsement of it all. Some writings are not worthy of serious consideration—as is to be expected in an area which so obviously lends itself to "crackpots" and straight-out deceivers. Serious ufologists themselves are only too aware of this regrettable problem.

Keel was amazed to find in that first year of investigation, 1966, that over 10,000 clippings and reports were sent to him. Throughout 1967 he spent a great deal of time going through masses of material, categorizing it and bringing it down to acceptable statistical form. He did not limit himself to reports of those who had supposedly witnessed flying saucers, but obtained all sorts of astronomical data relating to meteors. He even checked on rocket launchings, this information being provided for him by the National Aeronautics and Space Administration (NASA). In his fascinating book he gives a great deal of statistical information which no one else had come up with in quite the same way.

One night in March . . .

The reports continued to pour in. A typical sighting was that supposedly made on March 8, 1967, at 8:45 in the evening over Oklahoma. Mrs. Homer Smith claimed that she stepped on to her back porch and then "was astounded to see a twirling object with colored lights" that was overhead and moving toward the south. She called her young son and he too saw it, and they reported that colored lights were flashing out from it. On the same evening Mrs. Ned Warnock saw something from the kitchen window in Brikley in Arkansas. At first this object had a reddish-orange glow, then it changed to silver-white as it took off. She claimed that it was moving too fast to be a star. She alerted her neighbors and they also saw the object.

The same night Mrs. L. E. Koppenhaver reported that a big red ball traveled over her house in Iowa at about 9:54 P.M. She claimed that the object was moving very fast, much faster than satellites which she had seen before. She also stated that the UFO maneuvered very quickly.

Yet another report on the same evening was earlier, between 8:00 and 8:30, when police officers in Marion, Kansas, observed an unidentified flying object, and some of the officers even watched it through binoculars. They stated that it changed colors through red, green, and yellow. When this was reported in *The Marion County Record* on March 9, 1967, the report included the comment, "They all agree they saw it. There's no question about it." A similar sighting took place on that same evening in Kansas over Tawandra—a number of youths saw revolving red, white, and blue lights flashing in the sky. They called the marshal and he also watched the lights, as did a number of people who watched the maneuvering object from their motor cars. Trees were actually lit up by the reflection from this mysterious vehicle overhead.

John Keel describes 22 of these sightings on that one night—Wednesday, March 8, 1967. He makes the point that this was only a sampling of the sightings for that particular night, and that this was not an evening of exceptional flap. Most of these sightings were in the general area of Kansas and Illinois, following the pattern of a large concentration in the midwestern states, especially in less densely populated areas. Usually the sightings occurred between 7:30 and 9:30 P.M. when most people were at home watching television. When UFOs are sighted on the ground it is usually later than that—it almost seems that the vehicles land and conduct their clandestine operations in places and at times where the risk of observation is least. On the other hand, they do allow themselves to be seen, though they then usually disappear quickly. Some writers have suggested that this is part of their tactics—to be seen and reported by small groups, but not to be more fully investigated by larger numbers until their own time is ripe.

An "Innocent Bystander"

We have already referred to yet another remarkable "witness for the defense"—Dr. J. Allen Hynek, who was for many years a scientific consultant to the U.S. Air Force on unidentified flying objects. He says of himself:[14]

In my association with UFO phenomenon I was somewhat like the proverbial "innocent bystander who got shot." Project Sign needed an astronomer to weed out obvious cases of astronomical phenomena—meteors, planets, twinkling stars, and other natural occurrences—that could give rise to the flying saucer reports then being received, and I was the natural choice. I was then Director of Ohio State University's McMillan Observatory and, as such, the closest professional astronomer at hand.

We saw that before his investigations began, Dr. Hynek was typical of many who scoffed at the thought of flying saucers being real. He states that he had joined his scientific colleagues in many a hearty guffaw in what he termed the "psychological postwar craze" for flying saucers sweeping across the country. He was amused at the gullibility of so many of his fellow human beings who were taken in by what he regarded as "nonsense." He says that it was almost in a sense of sport that he accepted the invitation to look at the flying saucer reports, even feeling that he might be doing a service to help clear away "non-science."[15]

It is very interesting to trace the way in which Dr. Hynek himself changed over the years. Starting as one who had no serious sympathy with the "flying saucer phenomenon," he came eventually to a quite different point of view. As a scientist of integrity he found there was something that must be taken seriously.

Since the first edition of this book, I have been in personal contact with Dr. Hynek, who passed away several years ago. It was fascinating to talk with this remarkable man as he told me of his mental journey, despite his early skepticism. I appreciated his preparedness to stand up and be counted. His testimony is a strong pointer to the credibility of the witnesses and will be recounted in Chapter 16.

Chapter 3

Contact Is Made

So far, we have restricted ourselves to encounters where UFOs have been seen, either directly or on radar screens. However, the phenomenon does not end there, for there have been many reports of "close encounters" with the craft themselves, or with their occupants.

Some of these supposed encounters we reject as wild delusions or deceptions, but undoubtedly some are real experiences in the usually accepted sense of the term.

It is very difficult to know where the true and the false merge in the reports that are given. One "contactee" claimed he was told he was a reincarnated Saturnian, and before very long he had divorced his wife and married a girl who was supposed to be reincarnated from yet another planet. Most who read that sort of report would have serious reservations. Similarly, descriptions of George Adamsky and the "two incredibly lovely young women" would be regarded by many as no more than science fiction. There are other supposed contacts that many would accept with the proverbial grain of salt.

Dr. Hynek suggests there are three types of close encounters—"The Close Encounter *per se,* in which the observers report a close-at-hand experience without tangible physical effects; the Close Encounter in which measurable physical effects on the land and on animate and inanimate objects are reported; and the Close Encounter in which animated entities (often called humanoids, occupants or sometimes ufonauts) have been reported."[1] Dr. Hynek discusses representative cases from each category, choosing only reports that are from responsible people, when the contents of the reports were unexplained in "ordinary" terms.

This categorizing is interesting and valid, but we have not followed it, only because the pattern of this book is rather different from Dr. Hynek's. We shall glance at a number of cases which, if believed, indicate that contact is being made with earthlings. The possible consequences of this will be discussed in later sections, especially when we deal with paraphysical phenomena.

The Barney Hills Under Hypnosis

One of the stories most often repeated in UFO literature is that of Betty and Barney Hill.[2] One night in 1961 they were, so the story goes, driving along a highway when they were followed by a UFO. It landed when they stopped their car, and soon they were taken aboard the giant disk. They claim they were submitted to a long and thorough physical examination, apparently under hypnosis, and that then they were released with a post-hypnotic command to forget everything that had taken place. Their experience was followed by all sorts of headaches and emotional disturbances, together with bad dreams.

Later, with psychiatric help, they reconstructed their forgotten experience under hypnosis. A relatively recent report says that Barney Hill has died of a brain tumor, in his early forties, and that his wife has been seriously ill. Balanced saucer investigators believe that the incident did take place, more or less as the Hills reported, and have continued to insist.

Some have argued that this was a double dream hallucination, and that the incident never actually took place outside the mental realm. One major problem with individual cases is that subjective elements cannot be examined statistically. If this case were the only incident involving supposed hypnotism by the UFOs occupants, it could possibly be agreed that it was really some sort of hallucination. However, a major reason for taking the story of the Hills seriously is that there is now a mass of evidence that many other people have had similar experiences.

Undoubtedly some of those who claim to have had such experiences are publicity seekers, or "crackpots." Human nature is such that there are those who would invent fantastic stories and enjoy the subsequent limelight. However, many of those investigated have been reticent to tell about their ordeal because of the very real possibility of ridicule. Others could not possibly have known of the almost hidden similarities which only a careful investigator would uncover. There have been hundreds of such cases—some careful investigators would say thousands of them. John Keel discusses this at length in various sections of *UFOs—Operation Trojan Horse*. Over and over again he gives names of people, dates of happenings, and convincing details of investigation.

A Gap in a Patrolman's Notebook

Another convincing case involved a police officer— Patrolman Herbert Schirmer, who was supposed to have contacted the occupants of a spacecraft on December 3, 1967, in the town of Ashland in Nebraska.[3] Strange things were happening that night, with dogs howling in the darkness and even a bull kicking and charging at the gate of the corral in which it was held. Various unusual activities continued, with Patrolman Schirmer cruising around to see what was wrong. However, he found nothing until about 2:30 A.M. when suddenly the lights of his police car lit up an object on the highway ahead of him. At first he thought it was a semi-truck that had broken down, but eventually when Schirmer made his report he referred to an ordinary sighting of a UFO. That sort of sighting was relatively commonplace by then and did not cause too much excitement.

As one studies this incident, it becomes clear that it involved some frightening aspects. From the facts reported, there was a gap of several minutes in Schirmer's log book. He was put under hypnosis by Dr. Leo Sprinkle, and it is reported that the patrolman gave startling details of his contact with the occupants of the UFO while he had been under hypnosis in their vehicle.

As time went by, Schirmer found himself confused and psychologically disturbed. Eventually he sought help to find out what really had happened on that eventful night, partly because he wanted to get rid of the headaches that had persisted. Undergoing further hypnotic treatment he stated that at the time of the encounter his engine had stopped running and the lights on his police cruiser had dimmed out. He was unable to draw his gun, and he actually had some form of language contact with the occupants of the vehicle. They claimed they meant no harm to his people, and that they had landed in that area to take electricity from the power lines. He was told that their aircraft was operated by working against gravity, but he was unable to give details.

Despite a good promotion, Schirmer fairly soon resigned. He had taken a lot of ribbing about his seeing "green men from Mars," and he found that his headaches were getting worse. He was unable to do his police work effectively, and so he resigned.

According to published reports there were further hypnosis sessions, and he was able to recall other details, such as his own wondering as to what it could be on the highway ahead of him. He recalled that his radio did not work, and that both his engine and his lights had cut out. He described the object as being something like a football in shape, with flickering lights and a silver glow beneath it, and having tripod legs that shot out from the disk as it settled down on a nearby field. One of the spacecraft occupants had approached him and pointed something at him which gave out a bright light, after which he was paralyzed, and then blacked out.

When he recovered, one of the spacemen asked him if he was the watchman over the place, to which he replied he was the policeman. Questions were asked about power plants and water reservoirs, and then he was taken aboard the UFO. He was told that the vehicle operated by reversible electromagnetism, a process that enabled the craft to operate against gravity.

It is interesting to conjecture how these beings could communicate with Schirmer: according to the patrolman himself they did not speak with their mouths but communicated directly to his mind—some sort of mental telepathy. He reported that this made his own mind "hurt."

From Schirmer it was even possible to know some of the details communicated by these "spacemen" as to their own intentions. According to the published report, these people wanted earthlings to believe in them, and they were sending out reports, a little at a time, so that earth people would be prepared for them. They claimed that their purpose was not to conquer the world. Great detail was not to be given, and only a limited amount at a time.

The Patrolman Under Hypnosis

Under hypnosis, the examiners learned that Schirmer himself had been instructed to say no more than that the craft had landed on the highway, and that when he approached it, it shot into the air. This was, in fact, all that Schirmer reported, and it was all he remembered until he was put under hypnosis. He had been taken back to his police car, and the UFO occupants returned to their ship. Then there was a reddish orange glow together with a high-pitched whine, the tripod legs retracted, and the saucerlike vehicle shot straight into the air.

According to Schirmer he was told that its measurement was 102 feet in diameter. It was made from pure magnesium, and inside there were a number of computerlike machines. A large television-type screen could show pictures of what was happening outside, even though it was totally dark outside the UFO. Electricity could be drawn from nearby power lines simply by pointing one of the vehicle's antennae in that direction. He was also told that an electromagnetic field was used as a defense mechanism to surround the vehicle while it was on the earth. It was strong enough to stop automobile engines such as Schirmer's, and also to silence radios.

It is relevant to notice in passing that a number of other sightings have included references to electrical and mechanical interference such as this, on a considerable scale. Schirmer wondered if perhaps this caused the tingling feeling he himself experienced, and also the strange behavior of animals in the vicinity before he saw the UFO. Other reports have also told of people who have been burned by a white streak that was supposedly associated with a spacecraft.

The question could be asked, Why would such advanced vehicles need to take electricity in this way?

They have a problem in the actual storing of electricity, and so they take it from local supplies. In this particular case, according to Schirmer again, the electricity was actually put back into the power lines, and he stated that the dials of one gauge recorded when the electricity was taken and when it was later returned.

Schirmer's description of these beings is similar to that given by many other witnesses at other times and places. He claimed they were between four and a half and five feet in height, with larger chests than normal earth beings of that size. He saw only their faces, and they wore tight-fitting suits and boots, silvery gray in color. Their own skin was the color of dough. He described their eyes as shaped like cats' eyes, while their lips were more a slit in the face than like the full lips of humans. As we have said, these points of description have been made by many other supposed contactees.

Schirmer also claimed that inside the ship were a number of baby saucers which could be launched from the mother ship in order to check out the area. They could transmit both sound and sight messages back to the ship. He further claimed that the craft was propelled by reversible electromagnetic energy, and that this created an inertia-less gravity-free flight. There was a crystal-like rota that was located in the spacecraft, and he was told that this was linked to two reactors. By this system they could both control matter and overcome the force of gravity, enabling them to fly at fantastic speeds.

Underground Bases?

He even claimed that he was told where UFO bases were. Although he could not understand it, he stated there were UFO bases both underground and underwater. He wondered if perhaps these beings were careful to guard their own interests, for they gave no information that would actually endanger themselves. However, they did say that one base was out in the ocean away from Florida, out toward Bermuda. This is in the area of the infamous "Bermuda Triangle" where so many ships and even aircraft have mysteriously disappeared during this century.

Schirmer was further told that this particular vehicle was an observation craft, and that the occupants had been sent to collect samples of animals and vegetation. He remembered also that he was told that some humans had been used in breeding experiments. He was convinced that something was done to the brain patterns of those who were captured, and was definite that he himself had been changed—as was evidenced by his earlier withholding of details of the sighting. By his obedience he had become almost robotlike, ready to do whatever they told him to do.

Schirmer's story was supported, at least to some extent, by the physical evidence of that supposed landing. It was reported that pointed tripod marks were actually found in an unplowed field just above the highway where Schirmer sighted the spacecraft. Some of the grass in the field had been swirled into a pattern as though a whirlwind had attacked it, and some patches of twisted grass were dark as though they had been scorched.

This is not to say that the official report endorsed all that took place. In fact, a statement was issued that there was no evidence of a physical object being present as claimed, and that psychological assessment which had been carried out with the policeman's approval had failed to show that the reported object was physically real. However, the psychologist did report that the policeman himself believed in the reality of the events he described.

This does not rule out the validity of Schirmer's story, or of the evidence itself. Without intending to disparage official reports, there is some evidence to suggest that such reports are not always totally reliable, in that subjective considerations and prejudices are allowed to intrude. In Schirmer's story there are similarities to other reported sightings at various points, in ways that are not satisfied by a simple word such as "delusion." This is certainly not an isolated case.

Even some of the more startling reports cannot be dismissed lightly. One of the most bizarre at first seems totally incredible, yet, as it is carefully investigated, it is seen in a different light. At least let us glance at it objectively, without prejudging it with a biased "Impossible!"

The Strange Case of Antonio Villas-Boas

We have said that UFO reports are commonly made by highly reputable people. There are parts of the world where there is no longer a challenge as to the fact of UFOs—that is made clear by a report from Brazil dated November, 1966. At that time Dr. Olavo T. Fontes, Professor of Medicine at the Brazil National School of Medicine, made what at first seemed to be a surprising comment to newspapermen—that there was no flying saucer controversy in his country.[4] He went on to say that thousands of people had seen UFOs at close range over the previous sixteen years, and that there had also been a number of dramatic incidents. UFOs had actually landed, power supplies had been affected while these vehicles had been present, and numbers of people had suffered burns and injuries for which they required hospitalization. Dr. Fontes had investigated over 300 cases of reported sightings of UFOs and one of those whose story he told was of a young Brazilian farmer named Antonio Villas-Boas. He was supposed to have been taken aboard a flying saucer in October, 1958, apparently to engage in a breeding experiment with a female on board the craft.

It does not seem that Dr. Fontes was seeking publicity, for such a claim would certainly tend to reduce his own credibility. Nor does it seem that the young man, Antonio Villas-Boas, was seeking publicity, for he had little formal education and it is doubtful if he would have ever known what a UFO was, unless he himself had an actual experience of one.

At first Dr. Fontes was understandably skeptical about this bizarre incident, but then the young man broke out in a series of sores and yellow spots that suggested the possibility of some sort of radiation poisoning.

Villas-Boas has consistently told the same story of his seduction. Incredible as his account seems, he has been thoroughly investigated by a team of doctors and psychiatrists, and they have not rejected his story. Today he is married and works away at his farm, and has never looked for any fame or profit from his supposed adventure. In fact, he claims that he did not report it for some time because he thought he would not be believed.

Incredible? Yes—provided we date our writing to about 1950. In the 1980s we are forced to think differently, and to recognize that the incredible is credible after all. As with other types of contact, there are similarities in this record to those of other sex contacts with UFO occupants.

Contact by UFO occupants has been made, and if

the apparently reliable records are to be taken seriously, the bizarre has become the commonplace. It is frightening to consider, yet it is also important that we do consider it.

The case is established—there are some crackpots, some hoaxes, some publicity seekers, some who have been deceived, some who have done well financially out of their possibly true reports. However, the evidence strongly supports the fact, not only that the credibility of the witnesses is established beyond doubt, but also that contact has been made.

And with the release of so much secret material, the disturbing facts of contact can no longer be ridiculed. Rather they are cause of sober, disturbing concern. And even of terrifying anticipation.

Chapter 4

UFOs—USA or USSR?

Despite the credibility of so many witnesses, many writers and even defense personnel have remained skeptical. Obviously not all technological achievements are made public—and perhaps the UFOs were actually made in the United States or in Russia?

This possibility was put forward many times in the early days of UFO sightings—vehicles from outer space were unthinkable, and therefore it was considered that probably these were prototypes developed by the United States or Russia. However, evidence has accumulated in various ways to show that both those superpowers are mystified by UFOs—sightings have been made in Russia and the United States as well as in other countries, and no final solution has been offered.

Undoubtedly there have been UFOs made by earth powers. One single-seater hovercraft, called by the students who made it "The Skate," was exhibited in Moscow during 1970.[1] UFO literature contains photographs of USA craft also. However, though some aircraft with circular patterns have been made in the USA and other countries, UFOs as they are observed all around the world do not come from the United States or from Russia. Written reports make it clear that neither of those two countries is the source of the UFOs.

Foo Fighters and Other Craft

During World War II hundreds of American and other Allied pilots reported seeing so-called Foo Fighters—mysterious glowing objects that often appeared as they flew into battle. Sometimes they were seen singly, while at other times they were in formation. They paced bombers and fighters, and were able to out-do any maneuvers tried by those who attempted to track them down. The United States Air Force believed they were possibly some sort of a Nazi device, and when the war ended, this theory was thoroughly investigated. However, no trace was found of a Nazi secret machine such as these "flying saucers," and it turned out that the Nazi and Japanese pilots had been just as mystified by the Foo Fighters as the American and other Allied pilots had been.

Sensational reports have hit the headlines in the USA from time to time, such as that of radio commentator Henry J. Taylor, who claimed in 1947 that the saucers were American devices with a purpose that he could not reveal. Although some were guided, others simply flew around aimlessly in the sky. He claimed that most were made to disintegrate in the air but were harmless. The United States Air Force reacted by stating that there was no factual basis for Taylor's belief that the saucers were air force or navy weapons or devices. It was mentioned that his material had not been cleared with the U.S. Air Force.[2]

Another report was in *U.S. News and World Report*, which has a high rating in Washington. This claimed that the saucers were in fact secret navy weapons, one of these being a jet-propelled disk-shaped plane known as the XF-5U. In fact the XF-5U was not new at that time, and in any case it was propeller-driven, not jet-propelled. This identification with UFOs also was denied by officials of the United States Navy. They claimed that the XF-5U was never produced, though a model had been made. The White House joined in the debunking of these claims about secret weapons, but many ufologists claimed that this was simply a cover-up. Certain it is that the sightings continued to be reported.[3]

One report not denied was that the Avro Aircraft

Company was supposed to be building a flying saucer which would have a top speed of 1,500 miles an hour. There were hints that it somehow combined the forces of electricity, magnetism, and gravity for a revolutionary form of propulsion, though it was not electromagnetic propulsion as such.

Research personnel of various branches of the U.S. defense forces have suggested that the flying saucers were made by the United States, but were simply balloons such as the navy's Sky Hook Cosmic Ray Balloon, a huge plastic bag that at times would rise as high as 100,000 feet. Such claims have overlooked the fact that these flying saucers were reported over and over again as traveling at fantastic speeds, whereas balloons were relatively stable and went with the direction of the wind: flying saucers seemed to have no preference for going with or against the wind. In any case, another official statement made it clear that not more than 20 percent of the sightings could be explained by balloons of any type, including Sky Hooks.[4]

Donald Keyhoe quizzed Admiral Delmir Fahrney if there was any possibility that the saucers were in fact American guided missiles. Fahrney assured Keyhoe that the United States was years away from achieving anything like the performance of these widely reported vehicles. "And if we ever do match them, nobody would be crazy enough to test the things near cities or along airways. If anyone under me ever tried it, I would court-martial him—you ought to know that."[5]

It is obvious that missiles are tested in uninhabited areas or over the oceans—not in public places such as those where very often the saucers have been seen.

Another indication that these are not vehicles of American manufacture is that they can outpace high-altitude rocket planes. Major Robert White is reported to have sighted an object that flew alongside and then passed him when he was testnig an X-15 high-altitude rocket plane over 300,000 feet on July 17, 1963.[5]

The release of previously classified material now points to the genuineness of many such incidents.

The Astronauts Report . . .

Something similar was reported by astronaut Gordon Cooper, who saw a glowing green object approaching his spacecraft on May 16, 1963, while he was passing over Australia.

The first unmanned Gemini test in April, 1964, was supposed to have had four UFOs escorting it around the earth. Radar reports such as this would be accepted as irrefutable evidence in other less mysterious areas than the investigation of UFOs. The U.S. Air Force explanation was that these "objects" were in fact the booster that had been jettisoned from the launch vehicle, though in an earlier report it had been stated that the booster and the capsule itself came down as one unit, never having separated.

Astronauts Ed White and James McDivitt reported a strange object that was crossing their orbit when they were in space in June, 1964. This was at first explained by NASA as being the winged Pegasus satellite, but they later retracted this when tracking data showed that this satellite was over a thousand miles away at the time of the sighting.[7]

The *Herald* of Calgary, Alberta, dated April 1, 1969, reported that American astronauts had not only sighted UFOs but had actually taken photographs—the report being attributed to Dr. Garry C. Henderson, Senior Space Research Scientist with Fort Worth, Texas, Division of General Dynamics Corporation. He stated that astronauts had been instructed to say nothing about their sightings of UFOs, and that their pictures had been locked up.

Apollo 12 is supposed to have been accompanied by two bright UFOs on November 14, 1969—telescopes picked up one object behind it and one in front, and each object was said to be blinking its lights on and off rapidly.[8]

John Keel wrote an interesting article entitled "The Astronauts Report UFOs in Outer Space."[9] He quotes the actual words of a number of the American astronauts, and his survey adds up to a convincing argument that special interest is being shown by these "visitors" in the progress of space exploration by earthlings.

Clearly UFOs are not marked "Made in USA." They have frightening technological capacities beyond anything yet developed by even the world's greatest nation. Could it then be possible that the Russians have made some fantastic breakthrough? Do they have a secret weapon, fearsome in its dreadful potential?

The Russians Have Problems

However, even the Russians are supposed to have had their problems with UFOs in space. In March, 1965, their cosmonauts Belyayev and Leonov reported seeing a satellite they could not identify, and this was explained away by Moscow as being one of their own spy satellites. United States tracking stations were reported as stating that no Soviet spy vehicle had come close to the cosmonauts. Space writers argue that in fact a UFO accompanied that space vehicle from the Soviet Union.[10]

Pilots and other experts who knew the facts about technological achievements with aircraft were emphatic that the Russians could not have built flying saucers after the end of World War II in time for the great wave of sightings that commenced in 1947. It was often logically pointed out that even if the Reds had recovered from the tremendous pounding they had taken during World War II, and had stumbled on some amazing new method of propulsion, there would not have been time to manufacture them and then to have them shooting all over the world.

It was also emphasized that not one of these craft had been captured, nor had one crashed, so that its secrets could be extracted from the wreck. In view of the thousands of sightings all over the world, this would have been virtually incredible if the construction was ultimately to be credited to the Russians, or to any other earth power.

Others soberly pointed out that if the Russians had made such a fantastic technological jump by 1947, they most certainly would not have waited year after year before they made it clear that they were now able to control the world. The fact was that the mystery was worldwide, with credible witnesses in countries such as Europe and South America, the Far East, Canada, Australia, the Bahamas, Greenland, and even Antarctica reporting flying saucers. Foreign air force pilots and foreign airline crews were often involved in those reports.

At the time of the great "flap" in 1952, newspapers were persistent that they should be given more information from government authorities, especially from the United States Air Force. Where previously there had been amused scoffing, many editors were now demanding the answers to problems that clearly were serious. Many people believed that something was being hushed up. If so, what was it?

At the time of that flap, a number of newspaper reports suggested the possibility that the saucers were in fact Russian-built. Adding fuel to the fire was a semi-official report that a large disk had been found near Spitzbergen on June 28, 1952. Six Norwegian jet fighters were supposed to have had their radio jammed by strange interference; then as pilots circled, they described an enormous blue metal disk that was wrecked on the snowy ground. Several officers of the Norwegian Air Force were supposed to have landed in ski-planes, but no one was found aboard the disk, which was 125 feet in diameter and made of an unknown metallic substance. The story claimed that the disk was powered by forty-six jets around the outside rim, and that when these were operating, the outer rim rotated around the control unit which remained stationary. It was supposed to be found that its flight range was over 18,000 miles with an altitude range of 100 miles, and that it was equipped to carry high explosives. Then followed the statement that the instruments aboard bore Russian symbols.[11]

At the time, the story was not believed in United States Air Force circles, and when a routine check was made, the Norwegian government denied any knowledge of the disk's existence. Perhaps not surprisingly, there were many who said this was simply a cover-up, and there was much talk about the possibility of some fearful event beside which Pearl Harbor would seem child's play.

UFOs Over Russian Defense Centers

Another indication that UFOs do not originate from Russia is—as already stated—that the Russians themselves have been mystified by these strange intruders. There have been many seemingly authentic sightings of UFOs over Russian territory, and even over defense centers and missile installations. A typical report is as follows:[12]

> In the spring of 1959, UFOs brought near-panic to Soviet radar and air force personnel by hovering and circling for more than twenty-four hours above Sverdlovak, headquarters of a tactical missile command. The Red fighter pilot sent aloft to chase the UFOs away reported that the alien objects easily outmaneuvered their jets and zigzagged to avoid their machine gun fire.
> Dozens of nervous candidates for Soviet civilian flying licenses have complained about UFOs sweeping at them and even following their planes back to the airfields.

The writers from whom this quote is taken go on to give a number of other supposed sightings in Russian territory.

The fact that Russia has also had its problems with UFOs is not surprising, for these reports have come in the thousands from all around the world. There were great numbers of sightings in England and European countries in 1967, and in November of that year it was publicly announced from Moscow that Major General Porfiry A. Stolyarov had been appointed to head up an official UFO study project, launched by the Soviet government, and twenty Russian scientists were quickly recruited to help in this project.[13]

An interesting sidelight comes from Dr. Hynek. He is reported to have urged that the United States be the first people to make friendly contact with UFO pilots, if only to gain the secrets of their fantastic propulsion. If this knowledge was gained by Russia before the United States, Russia would be the dominant world power in a moment. One consolation is that ufologists would have us believe there is a cosmic law which would forbid the striving this would lead to between earth nations!

Strangely enough, one reason why the Russians have not made capital out of the flying saucer phenomenon is religious. Many have conjectured that the Russians would have used this as some sort of "cold war" tactic, but an interesting comment comes from *Radar News*. A report from Paul Vorohaef, a Russian now living in the United States, is quoted as follows:[14]

In southeastern Siberia unidentified flying objects have been spotted, causing great alarm more than a near-panic. This was interpreted by the Russian peasants as some awesome warnings of a Supernatural Being of some impending disaster, possibly the end of the world!

A Religious Fear

The editorial goes on to state that the Soviet press has said practically nothing about this possible invasion from outer space. According to Vorohaef, the reason is religious—that because of the fear of Russians turning to God, the Communists have done their best to squelch the reports.

This makes sense—if there is any truth in the paraphysical argument, as seems probable, it could indeed be a very real blow to the insistence on atheism, a "nonbelief" which is basic to communism.

If the answer to UFOs lies elsewhere—and centers around antigravitational forces or electromagnetism—their observed maneuvers indicate that they are a

"Mission Impossible" for both USA and Russia. We do not insist that the mission would be impossible as the centuries ahead are approached. Scientific progress and technical know-how will undoubtedly continue to take giant strides, and there may well be electromagnetic propulsion of such a nature that seemingly incredible speeds will be achieved. It is at least conceivable that antigravitational forces will eventually be utilized, with results that at present would seem virtually incredible and impossible of achievement. However, to suggest that either Russia or the United States of America has made such fantastic progress since the relatively primitive knowledge at the end of World War II is incredible. If that sort of advance had been made by either country, all the world would know—with such knowledge it would even be possible to hold the world to ransom.

To summarize: "Made in USA" or "Made in USSR" is not the answer. No earthly power could produce UFOs as they are reported around the world.

And as time goes by the mystery does not go away nor do countries around the world agree on any "natural" explanation. Indeed, there is no simple explanation. At least that can be made clear by the documents released under the Freedom of Information Act.

No. There is no simple explanation. Unless we accept the para-physical explanation put forward in this book.

But let's go on and consider some of those seemingly incredible contact tales.

Chapter 5

Incredible Contact Tales

When we first begin to read about the occupants of so-called spaceships, we are inclined to smile. We hear of beings less than four feet tall, and of others who are great monsters like apes. Some have Japanese-type features, while others have birdlike forms.

Despite initial skepticism, as the facts are studied it becomes clear that even these strange reports are more genuine than at first seemed possible. There was a strong tendency to ridicule these reports of little men in spaceships until 1954, when a large number of such reports were made in several countries around the world. As a result, even the sightings of monsters are now taken more seriously.

Occasional Hoaxes

Reputable investigators have researched hundreds of cases where people reported seeing various shapes and sizes of UFO occupants. There were indeed monsters that looked like apes, some that looked like hawks, others who were referred to as devil men, and even a moth man. Many of the witnesses were credible, and undoubtedly believed in the stories they told. Some exaggerated, and many of the stories grew in the telling. Others were plain hoaxes, and some "sightings" were even self-delusions.

However, the occasional hoax does not rule out other genuine incidents, and these have been widespread. In many countries of the world, in places where witnesses could not have had contact with each other, or have even read newspaper reports, there are such similarities that we are forced to the conclusion that "where there is smoke there is fire." Undoubtedly some sightings are real experiences in the usually accepted sense of the term.

Dr. J. Allen Hynek makes the point that the appearances of humanoids in association with UFOs are "backed by so many reputable witnesses that we cannot accept them as simple misperceptions."[1] He goes on to suggest that if this is some sort of sickness that affects only these strange people, it is hard to explain:[2]

Are these people all affected by some strange "virus" that does not attack "sensible" people? What a strange sickness this must be, attacking people in all walks of life, regardless of training or vocation, and making them, for a very limited period of time—only minutes sometimes—behave in a strange way and see things that are belied by the reliable and stable manner and actions they exhibit in the rest of their lives.

One hypothesis suggested by United States Intelligence was that sometimes there was a degree of factuality about the first stages of the experience, but that this was followed by hallucinations whereby the more grotesque elements were believed by those who reported the sightings. Officially, monster stories were ignored in the earlier stages of UFO investigation. It seems that part of the reason was that if it was admitted that such stories were being investigated, it would indicate that flying saucers were being taken seriously. Many officials believed that such an admission could lead to public hysteria.

"Contact stories" range over a number of types—sudden appearances in a room, or on a television screen when the normal program is blotted out, conversations alongside a grounded UFO, and even interviews and examinations inside the amazing vehicle itself. Some have claimed to visit other planets, and we discuss some of this varying material in the chapter on paraphysical phenomena.

Peculiar Telephone Calls

A number of those who have been "taken for a ride in a spaceship" have claimed that they felt both pain and cold in their genitals—one such was a prominent Brazilian lawyer, Professor Joao de Freitas Guimarares, a military advocate in Saõ Sebastiao, who insisted that he took off in July, 1957. His watch stopped during the time of his association with the saucer people, and many others who have had contact with grounded flying saucers have made this same claim.

We saw that one of the best-known stories of the UFO contacts is that of Barney and Betty Hill, and under hypnosis Barney Hill stated that he had been placed on a table after he had gone aboard a flying saucer, and something cold was lowered over his genitals. His watch also stopped during the time of his involvement.

A number of people have reported that after they had contact with UFOs they were subject to peculiar telephone calls. One such case was Philip Burkhardt, whose story is told later in this chapter. His wife reported that within a few days of the sighting they began to receive peculiar calls, with no one at the other end. At times the telephone would even continue to ring after the receiver had been taken up to answer the call. Their telephone bill showed a puzzling increase over what it had been in previous months. This might sound incredible, but John Keel discusses this at length to show that it is technically possible, and even probable, if UFOs are paraphysical manifestations.

Three separate quotes of many he gives are as follows:

She had been having unusual telephone problems and had also been receiving strange voices on her citizen's band (C.B.) radio.[3]
A telephone blackout next occurred—cutting off all of the participants from one another.[4]
There are now many cases in which the voices of de-

ceased persons have seemingly called up their loved ones on the telephone, just as the metallic-voiced space people have been phoning researchers and reporters around the world.[5]

Let it be noted that these quotations come from a reputable writer who had written a book, *Jadoo,* which took to task the mythical legends of the Orient, and had sneered at the occult. He had scoffed at UFO contactee reports, "but as my experiences mounted and investigations broadened, I rapidly changed my views."[6]

As well as telephone interference, other people have complained of inexplicable power failures in their homes at the times that UFOs were reported in their area. Others again have found their automobiles had temporarily lost their power.

There have been many other effects of a widely varying nature. Sometimes there has been a peculiar suffocating odor associated with the supposed monsters or little men, as the case may be. One incident, referred to above, dated to October 3, 1967. An aerospace computer systems engineer named Philip Burkhardt was alerted by two teen-agers to look at a machine hovering over the trees, a few yards from his home. He went into his house to get his binoculars, and when he spotted the vehicle again, he watched it until it raced out of sight. Air force officials questioned him for half an hour over the sighting, and, among other things, Mr. Burkhardt commented that there had been a peculiar odor, comparable to burning chemicals or electrical wiring, confined to the immediate area where the UFO had been sighted.[7]

Other contactees reported that afterward they found an oily substance on their faces, and sometimes on other parts of their bodies. Physical signs have often been found, such as red burning marks, swollen throats, etc., while some people have suffered from convulsions. We saw that large numbers have claimed that their watches had stopped, and in other ways there has been evidence that there was a period of time for which they could give no explanation. The frightening possibility is that they were under some sort of investigation, including hypnosis.

Reports of Spacenappings

There are also reports of kidnappings. Otto Binder recounts a number in *Unsolved Mysteries of the Past*, and such reports are widespread in UFO literature. One such story was widely printed in newspapers, and occurred on Christmas Eve, 1889, in Indiana.

The snow was piled up outside when eleven-year-old Oliver Larch was told to get some drinking water from the well. He went outside, and those who were still in the house—the Larch family and friends who were together for the Christmas season—heard the boy screaming, "Help! Help! They've got me!" The boy's father and some of the guests rushed out and were able to follow his footprints very clearly because of the snow. They could hear him crying over their heads, screaming out for help, and then his voice faded into silence. They could see nothing in the sky—as with so many modern reports of UFOs, whatever it was had quickly disappeared. Some UFO investigators believe that this lad was taken by saucermen, never to be seen again. Some go so far as to suggest that he was a specimen taken to check on how their breeding experiments were proceeding.[8]

A more recent report was of Telemaco Xavier who was supposed to have been abducted after refereeing a soccer match in Brazil in 1962. Reports indicate that a rubber plantation worker saw a saucer land, and that three men jumped out and forcibly abducted Xavier. The vehicle then took off at high speed, and later investigators found signs of a struggle where the spacenapping took place.[9]

Yet another case involved Rivalino da Silva from Argentina, supposedly abducted on August 20, 1962. His three sons Raimunda, Fatimo, and Dirceu watched as two silvery disks plunged toward the earth and then hovered for a while, just above the ground, while two orange clouds of smoke stretched from the vehicles and surrounded their father. Then as the two vehicles shot away at fantastic speeds into the sky, the screaming youngsters found that their father had vanished.[10]

In this particular case the police investigated da Silva's disappearance, and they discovered a sixteen-foot area that had been swept clean where the boys said the incident occurred. They also found drops of blood which had fallen into the soil. Another man came forward to say that the disappeared man had told him how three days before he had suddenly come across two little men who were only three feet tall, digging a hole. A remarkable point of similarity here is that many who claim to have had spacecraft experiences also seem to have had more than one experience, often with the first contact being of a seemingly minor nature, without any actual communication. Many such contacts have reported that headaches, dizziness, and even loss of memory followed their experience.

The fact is, da Silva disappeared from his home at a time that could be accurately pinpointed, and did not return.

It seems there are other authentic cases of attempted spacenappings that have failed, and this too is to be expected. There are large numbers of cases of people who refused to approach a strange disk vehicle, even though the invitation was given in apparent friendliness. There are credible witnesses who tell of strange beings about four feet six in height who attempted to abduct them, the contactees often being women—such as Ellen and Laura Ryerson who had a terrifying experience in a bean field where they were working at Renton, Washington, on August 13, 1965. They claimed that three saucermen about five feet tall with scaly skins and huge protruding eyes chased them, but they got back to their parked car and sped away.

Another case was in Argentina on October 4, 1965, when two young girls named Antonia Aparti and Adela Sanchez were on their way to school. They came upon some short creatures who they said only faintly resembled human beings. They reported the incident to their headmaster. He did not mock at them, for he had heard of a similar case two years previously.

There is even a story of a woman parachutist who jumped from about 28,000 feet in 1961, and the pilot of the aircraft from which she jumped saw her descending. He landed to wait for her, but she did not arrive. The story is that she floated down on her parachute three days later, and then claimed she had been captured in mid-air by a flying saucer, taken aboard, and eventually released.[11]

Animals and UFOs

There are also apparently authentic records about animals being "spacenapped," both in modern times and through the centuries. First, it is relevant to state that altogether apart from "saucer stories" there is very good reason to believe that some animals have visual and auditory perception greater than that of human beings.

There are many cases in literature where animals appear to have had some more alert perception of visible entities than human beings did. Brinsley Trench devotes a chapter to this,[12] linking some of the strange incidents of history—as with elephants and horses attached to the army of Alexander the Great, and going on to many modern incidents which he has culled from various writers such as Aimé Michel. He suggests that animals hear sounds that become unbearable to them, and so become terrified, as with Barney Hill's dog Delsey—often referred to in UFO literature. It became a cowering, trembling ball as the UFO experience commenced, and was still in that tense condition when the experience ended.

There are many records about flying saucers being witnessed, and the first indication of their presence coming from animals. Over and over again there are stories of dogs whining, horses stopping and refusing to go forward, stampeding among cattle, etc. Physical differences are relevant here—thus dogs can respond to a call on a high frequency whistle that would be quite inaudible to humans whose frequency range does not go so high.

One well-documented case relating to an animal and a UFO appears often in the UFO literature and dates back to 1897, to an incident in Kansas. It involved a former member of the state legislature, Alex Hamilton. Sworn statements by about a dozen distinguished people indicate that the incident is neither hoax nor illusion.

Going to investigate an unusual noise among his cattle, Hamilton saw an airship slowly descending. He called his tenant farmer and his son, and they seized axes and ran toward the corral where the cattle were secured. They claimed that the airship came to within fifty feet of the ground, and that they themselves were within fifty yards of it. They described it as being cigar-shaped, a description that fits many sightings today. It was brilliantly lit, with six strange creatures inside. The ship seemed to hover directly over a three-year-old heifer, and when the men went to her, they found a half-inch cable tied in a slip knot around her neck, with the cable then going up to the vessel in the sky. The cable had caught in a fence, and they got it clear. Then, the report states, "We stood in amazement to see ship, cow, and all rise slowly and sail off, disappearing in the northwest."[13]

This was before dirigibles had been invented, and the free-floating round balloons which were occasionally in the skies were quite unlike this huge 300-foot craft. At the time there were also many people who suggested that this unidentified flying object was in fact an airship that was being tested, and that the occupants were anything but visitors from outer space. However, there were hundreds of sightings, sometimes at the same times and in areas separated by great distances. One new airship could not possibly be the answer.

But it is noticable that these UFOs adapt to contemporary technology.

The Case of Snippy

Snippy was another possible animal-napping case. Snippy was Mrs. Berle Lewis's pet horse, and it disappeared under strange circumstances in September, 1967, from her farm in Alamosa, California.

Press reports at the time of Snippy's death are thought-provoking. They reached around the world— as shown by the story in the Melbourne (Australia) *Herald* of October 10, 1967. The pathologist stated that Snippy's abdominal, brain, and spinal cavities were empty when Harry King of Alamosa County in California found the remains of the horse after it had been missing for two days. There were ground marks similar to those supposedly left by UFOs in other areas, and the geiger counter reading was high.

At first the officials of Alamosa County tried to put the death down to lightning, but according to the pathologist who performed the autopsy, the absence of organs in Snippy's abdominal cavity was completely unexplainable—there were no signs of entrance to the body. "As for Snippy's empty brain cavity," he said, "there definitely should have been a good bit of fluid there." The report then states that the pathologist was unable to give any answer whatever as to the absence of material in the center of the spinal column—"This horse was definitely not hit by lightning," he is quoted as stating.

If we accept the worldwide reports, it is also true that many dogs have been taken, while in other cases the attempts have failed. Often all the blood has been drained from animals whose crushed bodies have been found soon after sightings, and with others all fluids have been drained from their brains and spinal columns. Reports often include dogs, but other animals such as horses, cows, chickens, and pigs are all included. It seems that cats are an interesting exception.

At least some of the gruesome stories about animal-nappings are only too true. What the purpose is, is difficult to assess. Some writers believe there is a limitation to the powers of these beings—that they need physical bodies to supplement their own powers. They apparently seek to find human bodies and human voices, but not human minds, for their own minds are sufficient once a suitable body has been "captured." Are animals a poor substitute, but better than nothing?

Animal Legends of Long Ago

Brinsley Trench has investigated records through the ages of animals being taken.[14] He suggests the possibility that some of the ancient legends of animals carried into the sky have a more factual basis than was previously thought. Truth is stranger than fiction, and in other areas legends are now recognized as having historical bases.

This could possibly be true with some of the folklore about animals, among tribes around the world. There is perhaps surprising similarity at times between the modern stories of animals disappearing into the sky and some of those legends that have been looked on by most sober historians as nothing more than the folklore of superstitious people, or even the deceptions of old-time rustlers who found an easy way to account for a missing sheep or bullock.

Perhaps in the case of animal-nappings there is some other fearsome activity, involved with the life principle when its final human form is inaccessible to these beings.

Ufologists would not all agree with this hypothesis, and they give various explanations for such activities. Some claim that these are biological tests, indicating that the space people are testing the native forms of life on a planet (earth) which they regard as one of their colonies. However, this explanation does not seem feasible. If we were to check out animals in a colony today, we would take further steps to eliminate disease, etc. If these happenings are to be taken seriously, there surely must be some other explanation.

There are many other stories involving living things —stories of space visitors supposedly gathering vegetables from private gardens, and also selecting flowers, grasses, barks, mosses, and other earth products. The stories do not end there, for even clothing hanging on wash lines, fertilizer, and farm tools are all involved in these supposed contacts with these little men from space.

There are limitations to their life-giving powers, and that itself would imply that their mission is impossible. Man is the master of the animals, and despite way-out theories such as monster insects waiting to attack us, man is still able to control the lesser beings. If through the long centuries of apparent sightings, animals have been part of the sinister plans of some hostile space people, again it must be concluded that the mission was impossible. Animals have not been transformed, not taken over by beings whose minds are totally opposed to man's welfare but having access to bodies of animals that are stronger than men.

If some such plan were seriously thought of, again we must conclude that the mission was impossible. The mission has failed.

These, then, are some of the seemingly incredible contact stories. Some of them become credible after all. What lies behind it all? Are the "visitors" hostile or friendly?

To answer that we must analyze certain other evidences.

Chapter 6

Friendly or Hostile?

Various arguments are put forward by ufologists to suggest that the spacemen are friendly to earth dwellers. It is often pointed out that they have not deliberately caused a single death among humans, though when this is argued, the apparent "spacenappings" of children and adults are conveniently forgotten. We shall see that other evidence is also put aside.

Then it is stated that despite their fantastic speeds, and their constant violations of our traffic laws, their spacecraft do not collide with our own aircraft. Those who put this argument forward are opposing the serious proposition of other ufologists that mysterious disappearances in areas such as the ill-famed "Bermuda Triangle" are also attributable to space activity. They also forget the supposed incidents of aircraft disappearing, of engines stalling, etc.—hardly "friendly" activities.

No Meddling in Political Affairs!

They also point out that the saucermen do not meddle in political affairs. However, these "visitors" do interfere in personal lives—brainwashings, kidnappings, etc., may not be "political" in the international sense, but they are a direct intrusion into personal liberties. Nations are made up of individuals, and interference in the freedom of an individual is similar in principle to interference at an international level.

An argument frequently used to show that the UFOs are friendly is that despite their tremendous power and their seeming potential for conquering earth, they have never done so. The other side is the possibility that all this is a lead-up to a great battle of the future—a veritable Armageddon. If the Bible is right about that last great battle, then, in ways that are not altogether clear to mankind, spiritual and human powers will be utilized. If there is indeed some massive program of brainwashing being carried out by these beings in flying saucers, the consequences could be terrifying.

Some have argued that if UFOs were friendly they would have landed in greater numbers and made formal contact, but others point out that over and over again they have been chased by air force planes and even by civilian jets, and that this could lead the occupants of the saucers to believe that we were the ones who were hostile. Others again have suggested that the evidence indicates they know our language, and if they were friendly they surely would have made much more contact. To this the answer is given that many messages have been passed on to "high authorities," and the oft-repeated claim is advanced that the authorities are keeping these things secret.

Another aspect of UFO "contact" is that no attempt has been made to answer radio signals sent out to them. Occasionally there have been reports of revolving lights or of lights that seem to blink at regular intervals. However, if these craft are manned by superintelligent beings, it is hard to understand why they have not answered radio signals. If they have the technological achievement necessary for space travel, they would also have mastered the techniques of radio reception and transmission. Monitors have not heard patterns of reception or transmission that are positively linked to spacecraft.

Another supposed pointer to the friendliness of these visitors is their extreme shyness—over and over again the reports tell of humanoid-type beings who disappear if their invitation to earthlings is refused, or who take immediate steps to remove themselves if they are discovered.

The Coming Cosmic Revolution

Many who regard these constant visitations as involving only friendly beings also believe there is the dawn of a cosmic revolution "just around the corner." Man is about to be directed from the twentieth to the one-hundredth century in a moment of time, guided by superintelligent beings, no longer muddling through on his own. Disease is to be conquered, health perfected, and old age eliminated. Planet-spanning transportation systems by teleportation are about to be introduced, with other technological advances which are so fantastic that they are even beyond man's present thinking. Welfare payments will be unthought of—they will be quite unnecessary. Our representatives to the councils of the united worlds will speak with one voice, totally representative of all the members of that interplanetary community who happen to live on planet earth. There will even be annual (perhaps bimonthly!) vacations to Mars and Jupiter and any other distant systems, according to the particular choice or interest of the one whose vacation is due. Earth itself will also be a center for space tourists, beings with whom earthlings will communicate by telepathy, without any trouble of having to learn a foreign language.

At times there are religious overtones that at first imply friendliness, with messages that have a surface resemblance to Christian revelation. However, the total picture is not of friendliness, for even when it has seemed that genuine "revelations" have been given, the evidence indicates that a pattern of deception has followed those earlier minor "prophecies" that have been of a fairly general nature. Even when those prophecies have been specific, it would seem they have been given as an inducement to cause greater belief in these strange beings. They in fact appear to be bent only on the fulfillment of their own plans, with no real interest in the welfare of those whom they contact. The contactees are merely instruments, to be utilized as much as possible. This does not necessarily imply any reflection or slur on the contactees themselves. All human beings would be considered "fair game" by these alien intruders.

Other ufologists, who suggest that the occupants of the UFOs are friendly, explain their lack of contact by the argument that they are superintelligent beings in some ways, but are lacking intelligence in others: they simply do not understand earth's people whom they are so carefully scrutinizing, analyzing and cataloging.

Others argue against this, suggesting that it is highly possible that the thinking processes of these people are different from earth beings: they might well be coldly materialistic, and would be utterly ruthless to achieve whatever their ends happened to be. Spacenappings seem to point to this. It might or might not be relevant to state that a surprising number of so-called contactees or witnesses of UFOs have died soon afterward—sometimes with leukemia, which can be caused by radiation poisoning. It is also thought-provoking to find, as one reads through the literature, that a number of those involved died at relatively early ages. This may simply be coincidence, and may be answered by the fact that UFO literature of this generation now covers a time-span sufficient for many to have died in the normal course of events. After all, death is a one-to-one appointment that nobody can fail to keep.

An Over-Crowded Earth

Others who advocate friendship with the space people point out that because man is on the verge of discovering ways of prolonging life for hundreds of years, in a relatively short time the earth itself will be so crowded that it will be essential to start colonies on other planets.

We have referred to revelations, and another supposed evidence of the friendly nature of the visits relates to the messages these spacemen give from time to time. Cosmic law is supposed to forbid direct interference in the affairs of people on other planets, but these outer space people (so the argument goes) watch the happenings on earth with alarm.

Some ufologists who argue this way point out that modern sightings have greatly intensified since 1947, and they suggest that this is a consequence of the 1945 dropping of atomic bombs over Japan. The theory is that this forced blasts of energy out into space, detected by sensitive instruments of superintelligent beings observing us from other worlds. Investigative expeditions have been sent to earth to warn the foolish inhabitants about the danger of continuing such activities. According to those who argue in this way, the messages given to contactees have centered on the problems that earth is facing if it continues to experiment with forces of nature in this way.

They also are supposed to show their desire for friendship by sending great balls of light into our atmosphere, thereby neutralizing the dangerous atomic radiation that results from the continuing explosion of atomic and other devices. The space people see our scientists poisoning the earth's atmosphere, and they in turn act as our big brothers by neutralizing the poison. Their friendliness is supposed to be toward all space dwellers, but they themselves fear the childlike earthmen who keep on exploding these dangerous nuclear bombs. We are not only sterilizing our own earth, but we are also sending up poisonous clouds that will penetrate other universes, and even lead to the destruction of other "innocent" worlds. So the argument goes.

Needless to say, some of the great achievements of ancient times are linked to this argument as to the friendly disposition of the visitors from space. They are supposed to have helped Noah survive the great flood, to have made it possible for humans to live through and beyond the ice ages, and to have given great scientific secrets to men throughout the centuries.

UFO Rescue Fleets

If all this is true, as many ufologists claim, there are great fleets of UFOs ready to evacuate the earth when some dreadful catastrophe occurs in the near future—possibly a dramatic change of the earth's axis which could lead to the elimination of the human race. Many ufologists claim that spacemen are standing by with thousands of machines, ready to save enough of their earth-colonists so that they will be able to re-launch an earth-type civilization on another space home already prepared for them. The words of Jesus about preparing a heavenly mansion are taken as pointing to this possibility. There are a number of adaptations and even distortions of the teachings of Jesus in space writings.

Some other arguments put forward are also not entirely unlike those of the Bible. The Bible teaches that the "old" earth will eventually be destroyed by fire, rather than by flood as in the days of Noah. Some ufologists argue that the earth is heading through space toward a deadly cosmic cloud, and that the radioactive outpourings will in fact cause the world to be destroyed by fire. Others suggest other possibilities leading to destruction—such as that the Antarctic ice cap will melt, leading to a rise of 600 feet in the level of the oceans, and thus inundate all the coastal areas of the world. Thousands of UFOs will be needed to rescue at least some of the earth's population, most of whom live in the lowland areas in relatively close proximity to the oceans.

Various dates have been given to contactees with UFOs, stating when the earth would be destroyed, but those dates have passed and the prophecies have thereby been disproved.

There are many others who do not see these visitors as having friendly intentions, for some of the bizarre incidents—incredible as they at first seem—have the same marks of genuineness to which we have already referred.

A number of reputable space writers tell the story of Lieutenant Cody and Ensign Adams, two naval officers who took off in a small blimp in August, 1942, maneuvering along the California coast on submarine patrol. They were checking against the possibility of Japanese attack. Their blimp was observed by patrol boats and fishing boats that watched it moving in to an area where there was a reported oil slick, and they were about to drop depth charges. As the astonished witnesses watched, the blimp suddenly shot straight into the air in a way that was not physically possible for its low-powered engines. It leveled off at about 2,500 feet, then drifted aimlessly for some two and a half hours until it came down on a California beach and fishermen grabbed its mooring lines. Everything inside the gondola was in perfect order, but the two naval men were not there. The blimp had been under close observation, and the men had not jumped or fallen. Nevertheless they had disappeared, and their bodies were not found.[1]

Similar incidents have taken place in peacetime as well. Among others, Otto Binder quotes the notorious case when a squadron of five Avengers, with a total complement of fourteen, flew out from Fort Lauderdale in Florida on a routine Atlantic flight. The war had ended, and so there would be no reason to think this was an attack from enemy forces. Some hours after they set off, an urgent radio call from the flight leader reported that the sky above and all around them seemed strange, and they were completely lost. The compasses had become unreliable and they could not tell up from down. Another garbled report in a hysterical voice stated that weird aircraft were closing in, and then there was silence. No more was heard from any of the five planes. A big Martin bomber with thirteen men aboard, equipped with electronic search devices, was dispatched to find the missing squadron of five aircraft. Not so much as a radio report came back from this plane, for it, too, utterly vanished over the Atlantic. The navy instituted a large-scale search with ships and planes, lasting three days, but no trace was ever found of the six missing aircraft or the twenty-seven airmen who had comprised the crews. The only possibility of physical evidence was that one survivor was reported to have been found in a rubber raft, virtually deranged as he babbled about weird airships that had abducted the others: he himself had managed to bail out and so escape. This story about a survivor is not officially substantiated, but certain it is that there is great mystery associated with the disappearance of those six aircraft and their crews.[2]

There are other stories of this nature, some of them quite bizarre, such as that of a jet plane being "swallowed" by a UFO in 1955. There is even serious conjecture that this could explain how a Russian satellite also disappeared mysteriously. In this connection ufologists have discussed the Russian communication satellite "Molniya-2." It was launched in October, 1955, and was expected to orbit the earth for many years. In April, 1966, NASA reported that it had disappeared unexplainably, and that this seemed to be contrary to the laws of science. UFO researchers suggested that in fact it had been captured by saucermen to be "dissected," so that firsthand knowledge would be gained as to human technological development. Perhaps it is relevant to state again that there are reports of UFOs being associated with satellites, both as they have been launched and then out in space.[3]

Those are seemingly strange stories but a possibly stranger one, repeated in UFO literature relates to a whole regiment of British soldiers who were kidnapped, or disappeared in some other way, in August, 1915. They were watched by twenty-two New Zealand soldiers who were in a trench not far away. The British soldiers were marching along when seven strange clouds appeared and apparently captured the regiment of soldiers, for when the clouds suddenly disappeared not one was left, and their fate was never known. At the end of the war the Turks claimed they knew nothing of this amazing "capture" on their own territory. This is another of those happenings that is taken seriously by credible UFO investigators, suggesting that at least sometimes modern researchers have produced patterns indicating that UFO occupants are hostile.[4]

Military Significance

We have already seen that one researcher who caused serious thought was Aimé Michel, who carefully studied a number of French sightings in the 1950s and suggested that the UFOs pursued straight-line courses across France. This led to many investigations, but it was found that the theory was limited and did not seem to fit all the facts on a worldwide scale. This is possibly because many more UFOs are involved than Michel himself had thought. However, it seems that within a 200-mile sector, sightings do follow straight-line courses.[5] This would possibly apply to specific UFOs, as with those studied by Michel. The overall pattern would be more diffuse.

Donald Keyhoe also writes of UFOs being potentially hostile, and shows how at times the sightings are apparently kept within particular state boundaries, even when those boundaries are not in straight lines. To him, the evidence suggested that some massive plan of mapping and strategic preparation was under way. This certainly would imply the possibility of hostile, not friendly, contact.

It has also become clear that there is a frightening pattern of UFO interest in defense areas,[6] with sightings over atomic energy plants, many air force bases, both in the United States and in other countries around the world, naval bases and marine air corps stations, the rocket testing base at White Sands in New Mexico, aircraft plants, and over most of the major cities of the United States. Other disturbing sightings have been made in many parts of the world, such as when two saucers circled around uranium mines in South Africa.

One frightening aspect is that many of the small saucers have been seen repeatedly over key defense areas, and if these small vehicles have been dispatched from outer space with such continuing accuracy, it would be reasonable to assume that larger vehicles could also be dispatched with the same accuracy.

Others besides Donald Keyhoe have written about the potential danger from UFOs. Dr. Hynek states that, from sources independent of his own official government investigation, it is known that UFO landings took place at Blaine Air Force Base on June 12, 1965, at Canon Air Force Base in New Mexico on May 18, 1954, and at Deerwood Nike Base on September 29, 1957.[7] There is the frightening possibility that UFOs are especially active in specific centers such as these because of their military potential for future operations.

However, this "continuing interest" is not limited to defense centers, for it can be shown that other centers also receive continuing attention. One example is that in the great "flap" of 1897, Sisterville in West Virginia was reputed to be one of the centers where a great "airship" was seen. In 1966–67, UFOs were still being seen regularly in that same center. Robert Wright, a leading attorney in that town, is reported to have stated that they had been turning up for months, usually on Wednesdays. He told how he and his wife had watched one from a high ridge that was visible from his office window. He stated that it seemed to split into three, "and all three of them took off like a herd of turtles."[8]

A Continuing Master Plan?

It is thought-provoking to realize that UFOs were reported in that area back in 1897, and that they were still being reported seventy years later, in 1967. It becomes clear that if there is some master plan involved, it does not apply only to a limited period such as that of an earthling's lifetime. Sightings have extended over much longer periods than that, stretching across centuries. It even seems that there are times of special activity, such as 1897, and then from 1947 to the present time. What coming events are casting their ominous shadows?

The sightings have been made around the world. Government authorities have been unable to do anything about these intruders in their air space, even when they have circled railways, forts, and other strategic areas. One such report describes the inability of the Swedish military authorities to do anything about unidentified flying objects that circled the fort at Boden.[9]

This and other similar incidents were investigated by John Keel, and he states:[10]

These investigations were apparently most thorough, for the Swedish, Finnish, and Norwegian defense departments took a very dim view of the whole situation. Their air territories were being invaded.

These sightings date back to 1934. Defense authorities could not explain the illegal air traffic over secret military areas. In fact, there is considerable evidence that governments have not known what to make of UFOs, and have at times considered that they might be hostile visitors who are not yet ready for an all-out attack. Many ufologists claim that governments have deliberately debunked saucer stories because they did not want the truth to be known. Even Captain Edward J. Ruppelt, who headed "Blue Book Project" from early in 1951 until September, 1953, wrote a book called *The Report on Unidentified Flying Objects*. He openly stated that he himself had qualms as to whether the whole project was simply a "front," designed to cover up another investigation of what the UFOs really were.

Captain Ruppelt had already publicly aired his views, including his uncertainty as to the intentions of UFOs, in an article in *Look* magazine. It carried a survey by a number of writers, entitled "Hunt for the Flying Saucer," prepared with air force help, and putting emphasis on the possible dangers which faced the whole world. It showed that sightings had taken place in the vicinity of many defense bases.

One evidence that the investigation was of a serious

nature was the conclusion to the survey, in the words of Captain Ruppelt. He himself was an aeronautical engineer, and had been a World War II bombardier. He had been assigned to coordinate the reports of UFO sightings and, where considered desirable, to make on-the-spot investigations. Captain Ruppelt summed up the situation at the end of the *Look* article in these words: [11]

> The only conclusion we have come to so far is that "flying saucers" are not an immediate and direct threat to the U.S. They have been around for five years and haven't struck yet. But that doesn't mean they are not a potential threat.

This article, together with the earlier article in *Life* magazine, caused a stir in official circles, and interviews with intelligence officers for publication purposes were forbidden.

However, though UFOs had not "struck," there was very real cause for concern. One of the most alarming sightings with overtones of apparent hostility took place on July 20, 1952, when two unidentified machines were reported over the White House in Washington, and a third near the Capitol. Various radar and other checks were made, and some amazing facts were ascertained—such as that one of these vehicles accelerated from about 130 to nearly 500 miles per hour in about four seconds.

UFOs Over Washington

This story of spacecraft hovering over key points of Washington D.C.—the very heart of the administration center of the most powerful nation in the world—is told in considerable detail by Donald E. Keyhoe.[12] He gives times, personnel, coordinations between the observations made at different centers, and details of how the machines could stop dead and then in a matter of seconds be speeding at a fantastic rate in the opposite direction, one stated speed being 7,200 miles per hour. There was even the very real possibility that the strange visitors were monitoring the radio calls being made about them, for the saucers apparently anticipated the directions in which the pilots would be moving.

It is no wonder this was regarded as extremely serious, for, as Keyhoe says:[13]

Up there in the night some kind of super machines were reconnoitering the Capitol. From their controlled maneuvers it was plain that they were guided—if not manned—by highly intelligent beings. They might be about to land—the Capitol would be a logical point for contact. Or they might be about to attack.

There was near-hysteria, and when the story broke there were revived fears that the Russians had some new secret weapons. Keyhoe quotes a Vickers expert who partly backed the possibility of it being a Russian machine by stating that, if the description of a machine sighted in the Soviet zone of Germany was accurate, it could have been a military hovering craft. One of the London newspapers had tied this description in with the incidents over Washington, and American commentators repeated the story. They left unanswered the question as to the possibility that Soviet spotting devices were marking out key American bases and centers for later attack.

The first Washington incident was on July 20, and on July 26 there were other incidents that caused alarm, including a sighting over the naval air station at Key West. On that same night, sightings were again made over Washington, confirmed by officials in the towers at Andrews Field and also Washington Airport, these sightings being in confirmation of simultaneous sightings by airline pilots.[14] Newspapers across the country attacked the air force, claiming that if these were secret military experiments it was foolish to maintain the efforts to shrug them off, or to insist that details could not be released. National sanity appeared to be at stake.

A further news conference was held, in which high air force officials did their best to debunk the whole concept of flying saucers. One of the arguments was that 75 percent of the so-called sightings could be explained, and it was not unreasonable to expect that the other 25 percent would also be explained, either when knowledge increased, or if all the facts became known. However, conferences could not resolve the continuing problem, though they did help to allay public fears.

The Infamous Bermuda Triangle

We have seen that a number of writers have suggested that the mysteries of the infamous Bermuda Triangle are linked with hostile UFOs. In that so-called triangle, going around the coast of Florida and the Bahamas, there are many still unexplained mysteries of ships and aircraft disappearing without trace. A number of theories have been put forward, such as the influence of magnetic fields and various geological features, and these could well be relevant. Another theory is that there are UFO bases on earth, and that this is one of their major areas.

One frightening aspect is that UFOs do appear to have certain basic areas—referred to as "windows" by ufologists—where they are seen much more frequently than in other places. The Gulf of Mexico is the center of one such window area, stretching out to include Mexico, Texas, and the southwest states of the USA. Other windows are directly over the areas of magnetic deviations in the United States. Some ufologists believe that this points to hostile intentions: a number have put forward the claim that earth is being thoroughly mapped, with a giant plan in hand, of which we are only partly aware.

If UFOs are indeed hostile, we can only conclude that their mission is impossible at various levels. Sightings have taken place now for thousands of years, and, whatever the reason for their interest, earth has not been invaded. If by "hostile" we mean a force capable of physically taking over earth, its people, its installations, and all else that we think of as part of our social, cultural, economic, and even military environment, we are justified in concluding that their mission has failed.

Chapter 7

Sightings Through the Centuries: And the Chariots Still Crash

At the close of our last chapter we said that sightings have taken place for thousands of years. Much has been written on this topic—some of it quite unacceptable and distorted. Nevertheless the phenomenon is not new, and the seemingly incredible pattern through ancient times is in some ways similar to modern incidents. One adjustment to our thinking is necessary: we need to recognize that these beings have adapted themselves to different ages and cultures. Their manifestations and actual appearances in the pre-space age are somewhat different from those of the late twentieth century.

As with modern reports, we read these ancient records somewhat critically—where do truth and fiction merge? To what extent has the story grown in the telling? Was it a "real" observation or a mental delusion? Was it a mirage or one of the other "natural" happenings? We do not always know, and we do not necessarily accept all the stories and reports that now follow. However, they are relevant, if only to show the similarity to modern happenings, demonstrating a continuing phenomenon. Later we shall ask questions as to the nature of the phenomenon itself. In this chapter we shall restrict ourselves, in the main, to the reports of sightings before those of this generation.

An Anchor to a Church

There are many records of ancient sightings. An interesting one dates to the first century A.D., and is found in old manuscripts.[1] The story is that an anchor dropped from the sky and attached itself to a church steeple in Cloera, Ireland. The people of the town reported that they saw a vehicle in the sky with men aboard. One man is supposed to have climbed down the cable, apparently to release the anchor, and those who watched described him as though he was swimming in water. Some of the crowd wanted to climb up the steeple and capture him, but the bishop restrained them. Soon the odd-looking humanoid returned to his craft, without finishing his task, the cable was cut, and the vessel vanished in the sky.

With his great penchant for research, John Keel has dug out a very similar story, quoting an ancient Irish manuscript, the *Speculum Regali*, dating to A.D. 956.[2] Again a metal object was dropped from the sky with a rope attached, and it caught in an arch above the church door. When the people rushed out of the church, they saw a ship with men on board, floating at the end of the anchored cable. A man leapt overboard and moved down the cable to the anchor as though he would unhook it. The people rushed up and tried to seize him, but this bishop also forbade them from holding the man for fear it might kill him. When the man was freed, he hurried up the cable, the crew cut the rope, and the ship sailed out of sight. According to the Irish story the anchor was retained in the church as a testimony to what had happened. Is it the same story updated?

Yet another church in Bristol, England, was supposed to have had a unique grille made from another anchor that dropped down from the sky about A.D. 1200. Once again a mob of churchgoers gathered round to watch as a sailor came down the rope to free it. In this case the visiting sailor was supposed to have suffocated because of the moist atmosphere, and died. His unseen comrades overhead cut the rope and took off, but the anchor remained behind as in the other stories, and was installed on the church doors.

It is relatively easy to dismiss these stories as updatings one after the other, but such "updating" is unlikely unless there has been a tremendous amount of research done in outlying centers. It could be that the same ruse has been repeated to convince men that there are superior intelligences "way out there." The discussion as to who they are is left until later in this book. However, if we accept the reality of these stories, perhaps the pattern can be understood. These unidentified flying objects have appeared at many different times through the centuries, adapting themselves to the state of knowledge of men on the earth at that time, even repeating their own actions and demonstrations—such as the dropping of an anchor on to a church steeple from a spacecraft. If the activity achieved its objective once, why not use it again?

Ancient Spacenappings

A story with some similarity is recorded in the *Daily Chronicle* of Muskegon in Michigan, dated April 30, 1897. A huge vehicle is supposed to have hovered over the town of Holton, visible for nearly an hour. Then it moved off, but as it did so, a grappling hook was let down and carried off one of the town's reputable citizens. He is supposed to have come back by train the next day. This particular case may actually refer to the one airship that had been built at that time, if the report is to be taken seriously at all.

Not always were such stories of "spacenappings" taken seriously, nor were contactees' stories always believed—as with many modern sightings. People are more tolerant these days, and the penalty is usually no worse than ridicule. However, it has not always been so. Through the centuries—if the record is right—some have been killed because of their supposed association with space people, one example being in a discourse written by Compte de Gabalis in 1670. He states that during the reign of Charlemagne, about 900 years before his own time, a ship had come down from the sky and taken three men and a woman off into space. Some years later the craft is supposed to have returned with the people who had been spacenapped, and then these persons told a wonderful story of where they had been outside the earth. They were stoned to death for being "in league with the devil."

There are other records of flying saucers in ancient records.[3] Modern UFO literature quotes many such sightings—a flying lance in A.D. 577; a supposedly elegantly shaped ship with marvelous colors in the sky in A.D. 1254, and a revolving wheel accompanied by a barrel of flame over England in 1387. An astronomer named de Rostan was supposed to have seen a vast object in the shape of a spindle crossing the sun on August 9, 1762, at Lausanne in France. There are a number of astronomical sightings of strange objects in the sky during the nineteenth century, sightings which authorities claimed could not be attributed to meteors. There were also sightings of lights that advanced through the clouds, associated with a larger cloudlike vehicle.

A UFO at Niagara Falls

There was a burning torch and glistening balls over Hungary in 1819 and an aerial burning torch was over Italy in 1898. Other sightings have been of luminous bodies that rose mysteriously out of the sea, such as that seen by the brig *Victoria* in the Mediterranean Sea on June 18, 1845. It is supposed to have remained in sight for ten minutes before it disappeared. It was earlier claimed that thousands of people on both the Canadian and American sides of the Niagara Falls saw a strange vehicle shaped like a square table, hovering over Niagara Falls for an hour in 1833.[4]

On February 28, 1904, the USS *Supply* reported

three "remarkable meteors" that appeared over their ship and stayed there for two minutes; meteors would have disappeared in a matter of seconds.[5]

Serious space writers refer to various other mysterious incidents, some of them quite bizarre—such as a jet plane being "swallowed" by a UFO in 1955. On the surface this seems incredible, as though it should be taken with the proverbial grain of salt. However, this is a mystery that has gone beyond a simple explanation such as "an unobserved crash."[6]

Some even tie the many "water sightings" in with mysterious stories of ships that have vanished without trace. In *Unsolved Mysteries of the Past*, Otto Binder suggests that this could be the answer for famous cases such as that of the *Marie Celeste*, found adrift near the Azores on December 5, 1873. The sails were fully set and the ship was moving, but there was nobody on board. The last log entry dated to November 25 and it did not give any hint of trouble. Nobody ever again heard of the fourteen crewmen.[7]

Another example he gives in that same context is the French ship *Rosalie*, sailing to Havana from Hamburg, and found abandoned on November 6, 1840. The valuable cargo was intact but there was no clue as to what had happened to the missing crew. Certain it is that an unusually large number of ships and even aircraft have vanished without trace in the Bermuda Triangle area, which many ufologists believe is one of the major UFO centers of activity—a "window" area.[8]

We saw that a great number of sightings occurred in 1897, and that this so-called flap has often been put down to an airship that was being tested. We pointed out that UFO investigators have found that sightings of the "airship" actually took place on the same day over dozens of widely scattered areas—there was not one ship, but a whole fleet of them! Yet it is strange that once again there was an adaptation to current events and knowledge.

Activities in Cuba

That is illustrated by some of the supposed messages given during the year 1897. One report came from "ex-Senator Harris" who had a long discussion about such matters as the hostilities in Cuba with an elderly gentleman from an "airship." The story was published in *Modern News* at Harrisburg in Arkansas, on April 23, 1897. The same conversation included a reference to the Armenians, who at that time were being badly beaten by the Turks. The Cuban crisis referred to was one of the preliminaries before the Spanish-American War, and if this was a genuine contact, it again indicates that the occupants of these vehicles knew a great deal about contemporary events.[9]

Another reference to those activities in Cuba dates to that same year. The *Argus Leader* of Sioux Falls, in South Dakota, on April 15, 1897, told of a sighting in which the occupants of an airship had landed to make repairs to their vehicle, and told some farmhands who approached them that they would "make a report to the government when Cuba is declared free."[10]

There are many such reports of spacecraft making repairs to their vehicles. Over and over again, parts drop off, and it almost seems that the UFO occupants are anxious for contactees to believe in the physical nature of their vehicles. If these beings do indeed come from outer space, and if there are the tens of thousands of UFOs that would be necessary to account for the worldwide sightings, obviously they would be super-machines, not regularly breaking down in such unlikely spots—just where they were sure to be seen by earthlings. It seems there is a deliberate attempt to make sure that their totally material nature is really believed in. Why? Is it, as John Keel suggests, "a cosmic hoax"?[11] Is it to turn people's attention away from the *real* danger? As we proceed, we shall see that old issues need to be faced in a new way, by scientists and all members of society, and even by theologians.

Potatoes from the Sky

It is even possible that the objects, etc., dropped from the UFOs through the centuries have been deliberately adapted to suit particular time periods. In the great "airship" flap of 1897, the objects were such things as newspapers and peeled potatoes. More recently there have been globs of a purple oil-like substance, which would help to give the impression that these were modern supermachines, not mere hallucinations or illusions.

Whatever the explanation for UFOs, if their reality is accepted, then some of the strange stories of history will also be taken more seriously. Stories such as fish and flesh, and ice and stone, falling from the sky have not been taken seriously by most people, and yet when investigated, they have all the hallmarks of actuality.

A typical writing-off relates to the modern examples of massive blocks of ice falling from the sky.[12] Debunkers have insisted that they fell from airplanes—that water from wash basins had formed ice on the underside of the fuselage, and the plane had then flown into a layer of warmer air, causing the ice to fall off. However, weather reports at this and other times have "defused" this explanation.[13] In any case, these things have been reported long before the existence of airplanes as we know them today. To suggest that it is merely water forming into ice, then the plane running into warmer layers of air is not convincing, nor does it begin to explain the many incidents of masonry and other strange objects falling out of the skies.

Astronauts have seen very few objects in space that could be called rocks or meteors, yet undoubtedly many rocks have fallen from the sky through the centuries—there are many such reports. Animal and vegetable matter of several varieties have rained down in many unexpected places. Certainly not all of it is explainable by a wise nodding of the head, and a declaration in one word such as "whirlwind" or "hurricane."[14]

It is at least possible that these things should be linked with similar activities of spiritists where rocks and other objects have materialized in rooms, and in remarkable quantities.

We have referred to adaptations through the centuries. Another example of possible adaptation to modern conditions relates to an incident occuring on October 11, 1966 when a brilliant light was observed over the Wanaque Reservoir in New Jersey. This had been an area of many previous sightings but on this occasion no less than seven helicopters appeared and circled low over the reservoir. Then approximately ten jet planes arrived. The area was soon packed by lines of cars watching the strange phenomenon, and air force bases, airports, and the Pentagon itself denied knowing anything about the origins of the planes and helicopters.[15] Even the Civil Aeronautics Board was unable to throw any light on the mystery.

Either a very large number of witnesses were totally deluded, or telling lies, or there was some sort of adaptation by UFOs to this particular time period when helicopters and jet planes were "in," rather than, e.g., the airship of 1897.

Interestingly enough, these mystery helicopters were again seen in the state of Maryland on Tuesday, August 19. There were many witnesses as seven "helicopters" hovered overhead near the Rosecroft racetrack, near Phelps Corner in that state. There was even a report of a "nonexistent" helicopter being shot down over Vietnam in 1968. This last incident of a single helicopter might be more easily explainable than the others.

The point is that there are demonstrable similarities between ancient and modern sightings. The shapes might change—for the crafts seen in the 1980s certainly are not the 1890s models. But there is an eerie, overriding similarity. Beneficence is used to hide ultimate evil, implanted knowledge to gain acceptance—and we must not be deceived.

The Amazing Knowledge of the Ancients

Ufologists at times make much of the great knowledge of many of the ancients, and suggest in all seriousness that their secrets were given to them by spacemen. One such claim relates to Johannes Kepler, the astronomer who first described the possibility of the planets orbiting around the sun. He wrote a fantasy relating to a space trip which is astonishingly accurate in details, and involves principles of space flight that were thought to be unknown when he lived (about 1600 A.D.). Otto Binder points out that Kepler speaks of the shock of acceleration, of protective suits that would be worn by the crews of spacecraft, and of other matters such as achieving free fall in orbit and the human body becoming weightless in space.[16]

If Johannes Kepler did indeed have this information from some source outside himself, it possibly should be placed in the same category as messages through mediums and clairvoyants. This would not necessarily indicate that the information was inaccurate. We see throughout this volume that many of the messages given from so-called spacemen in modern times have been accurate, even involving prophecies, but over and over again it would seem that sufficient information of an accurate nature is given so that a greater message is also believed, but that this does not always prove to be accurate.

It is possible that Kepler's terminology and knowledge could to a great extent be attributed to his own capacity and foresight as an astronomer. If this is so, it would mean that his observations and conclusions could have led to hypotheses such as that human bodies would be weightless in space, etc. Many writers would not agree with this conclusion, and they may well be right, for there are other well-documented examples of amazing knowledge being known long before we moderns would have expected it to be known. However, it is entirely possible that some of that knowledge has been gained from many different sources. Dr. Hynek comments that Kepler, "unable to garner data himself, used data obtained throughout the years by the Danish astronomer Tycho Brahe . . ."[17]

Another remarkable example quoted by space writers is Cyrano de Bergerac, who wrote about 1650, describing a machine that was propelled by three rocket stages. The same man wrote about permanently burning lamps, a description which seemed to point to electric lights; of talking books, which might well have referred to radios; and of people's faces that were seen on a monstrous pearl, which is rather like what we have with our modern television.[18] Was it good research? Imaginative writing? Or was he given information from nonhuman sources?

There are a number of writings during the Renaissance period where professional people testified to long conversations with strange people who helped them discover various scientific principles. It is possible that this sort of writing is simply a literary device, and if so it should always be taken in the sense in which it is meant, merely indicating that the knowledge is beyond the writer's own understanding. However, even if these Renaissance writings are following a pattern of accepted literary practice, they may still be following a pattern based on actual incidents. Through the ages, even going back as far as to the famous Chaldean astronomers, there have been descriptions that seem to go beyond the knowledge of those particular times. Some of those men of old were surprisingly knowledgeable.

Nevertheless it is also true that some ufologists claim too much for the ancients. They declare, for example, that as long ago as 5000 B.C. Chaldeans actually had blueprints for the manufacture of UFOs. With all that we hear from some ufologists about the great achievements of these early peoples who were supposedly helped by men from space, it is hard to understand why they did not actually make these craft if they had the blueprints.[19] Undoubtedly there was speculation as to the possibility of vehicles that could fly through the air and even into space. However, that now-accomplished dream was still a "dream" in very recent times, until the advent of the airplane. As well as being the dream of men of old, it was the "dream" of modern man too.

Men of brilliance—even genius—have lived through the long centuries, and it is to be expected that discussions about flying and even space flights would be found in the records of the ancients. Scholars would not doubt the possibility of men writing about spacecraft and space flights only a hundred years ago, but we tend to forget that even then these things were still in the realm of fantasy, before the Wright brothers helped to usher in the modern era of flight.

Undoubtedly early people had fantastic knowledge—thus we read that the Chaldeans knew there was another planet besides Mercury, Venus, Mars, Jupiter, and Saturn which were more easily seen. This knowledge was not confirmed in modern times until 1781 when William Herschel picked up Uranus with a powerful telescope[20]—before that time it could only be observed as a seemingly "fixed star" rather than as a moving planet.

It is not possible to explain all ancient mysteries, or to tell where all ancient knowledge came from. The time barrier has not been broken for many areas of knowledge, and with all our advances there is still a great deal to be recovered. Archaeology has done much, and will do much more yet, but it would be naïve to expect all gaps in our knowledge to be filled as archaeological techniques improve and research continues.

There will always be mysteries. The facts of the case make this clear, for it is obviously impossible to go back and record conversations, attend "board meetings," or even check on the minutes of the meeting. We have no "time-crossing" telephones, and much of the past is forever buried. In fact, it is amazing that so much *has* been recovered, for as one level of occupation succeeded another, the earlier level, lower than the new one, was virtually destroyed or became the foundations for the new level. There was not always the interest there is today in earlier civilizations, and there was not a great deal of exploration of the past—when compared with modern excavations.

Because there are necessarily gaps in our knowledge, a door has been opened for romantic writers to theorize and to conjecture—sometimes more or less sensibly, and at other times not so sensibly.

These theories come and go, usually making little more than a ripple before they are forgotten. Occasionally a combination of circumstances causes a particular theory to be more widely accepted than others have been, and we have witnessed a recent example of this in Erich Von Daniken's *Chariots of the Gods?*.

He takes many of those seeming mysteries of the past and brings them together with what to many has seemed a convincing explanation. His solution is that ancient structures were built with the help of visitors from outer space. At first reading, some of the hypotheses seem plausible, supporting his major argument.

However, as we continue reading, doubts arise, for it becomes clear that some of his evidence is not so convincing after all. He too readily "presses a button" and an astronaut conveniently appears.

In the main, the approach in this book is radically different from that of Erich Von Daniken. He deals primarily with supposedly unexplained mysteries, and he is very forceful in his suggestions about the contacts that beings from outer space have had with earthlings. However, there are areas where it would appear that his approach blends with the approach of the present writer, and for that reason it is necessary to consider briefly in what ways *Crash Go the Chariots* is diametrically opposed to *Chariots of the Gods?*.

The Chariots Still Crash

Crash Go the Chariots dealt especially with two major aspects of Von Daniken's writings—firstly his challenge to archaeology and archaeologists, with his consequent rejection of many of their conclusions; secondly, his erroneous references to Bible records. As one who has been a practicing archaeologist and has lectured in Bible history for many years, it seemed appropriate that this author should challenge a number of Von Daniken's way-out hypotheses, conjectures, and conclusions: hence *Crash Go the Chariots* was born.

In a radio interview in Australia, Von Daniken stated that a number of his arguments were put out deliberately to be provocative. If he was being provocative in stating that so many mysteries of the world were explained by one visit from outer space, his argument becomes nonsensical, for many of the things to which he refers are separated by literally thousands of years. As we read his books, we find he produces astronauts as the answer to many apparent mysteries—weaving a semblance of connections between incidents that are in fact not connected except in his highly imaginative presentation. In that same interview, he was asked where the spacemen were now, and he stated that they must still be returning to their far-distant space home. This concept of one visit is in direct contradiction to the many regular visits which are required for *Chariots of the Gods?*.

Von Daniken's books have been criticized in other writings besides *Crash Go the Chariots*. Reverend Gordon Garner, director of the Australian Institute of Archaeology, provides a telling critique in his *Chariots of the Gods? A Critical Review*.[21] Yet another who reviews *Chariots of the Gods?* is Janet Gregory, in *Spacelink*.[22] She refers to how well the book has done financially, but then she says she is only partly convinced of its value. She mentions that fabulous facts tumble over themselves in their haste to amaze you, and suggests that the impression is finally one of unreality, though this was never the author's intention. She states:

All the data cited fits too neatly into the jigsaw, so that in the end one mistrusts the information. Also, from experience, I have found that the real experts can often give logical, sane and, more important, mundane explanations for much of what is churned out again and again as "evidence" of extraterrestrial visitations. I felt that Von Daniken's tirade against conventional archaeologists was overdone, and certainly not called for.

She concludes on the note that his material is not new.

It was refreshing to read that Von Daniken's tirade against conventional archaeologists was not called for. Clearly UFO writers do not all accept everything that Erich Von Daniken has written. This does not only apply to *Chariots of the Gods?*. In the April, 1971, volume of *Spacelink*, his book, *Return to the Stars*, is reviewed by Colin Bord, and among other statements he comments:

Facts, theories and speculations are piled up page upon page, but the ultimate effect tends to be chaotic and intellectually undisciplined.

Von Daniken's third book, *Gold of the Gods*, is challenged in similar style. He makes much of great quantities of "gold" that he saw stored underground in Ecuador. The "gold" was bronze. Other supposed facts are challenged in *Anatomy of a World Best Seller* published in *Encounter* (London), August, 1973.

Erich Von Daniken's writings have been seriously attacked even within the camps of ufologists—there is clear recognition that he has gone too far in many of his claims. Sensationalism and adaptation of facts occur so often in his books that many who might have taken these matters seriously would tend to decide that the whole matter is not worthy of serious consideration.

In *Crash Go the Chariots* we show that Erich Von Daniken makes many conclusions which are not supported by the facts. He belittles archaeology and archaeologists, and simply weaves an apparent connection where those connections are not justified. He jumps from hypotheses to conclusions in a way that is unacceptable to men of science. Thus many of the historical incidents that he sees as being explainable only by UFO help are satisfactorily answerable by more usual activities and processes. This does not alter the fact that, if we can believe that UFOs are real today, there could be some aspects of early history which might have involved knowledge gained from sources that were not human. This we have referred to earlier in this chapter, and we elaborate on it here and there in the last three chapters of the book.

At the same time it should clearly be stated that it is quite unjustified to claim that the great engineering feats of the ancients can be explained only in terms of spacemen visiting earth. There are remarkable engineering and other feats associated with our forefathers. There are also highly developed technological achievements for which the processes are still unknown—experts still cannot give all the answers for some of those early achievements. However, despite their magnitude, some of those activities were certainly within the capabilities of human beings, often using surprisingly simple techniques and equipment.

No UFOs or Levitation at the Pyramids

In *Crash Go the Chariots* we show that the pyramids of Egypt were fantastic constructions, and the greatest of the pyramids would be so recognized even by today's standards. Explanations can be given for their construction, and the evidence shows that the Great Pyramid could be built in a relatively few years (as the historian Herodotus had stated)—not needing 644 years as Von Daniken claimed. Nor would levitation be required—a possibility suggested by Von Daniken and others—utilizing some antigravity force whereby huge blocks of stone could be maneuvered as though they were without weight.

No embalmed mummy has been recovered at the Great Pyramid, and it is possible that it was not a tomb as such. Whatever it was, it certainly utilized very great astronomical knowledge, indicating that these learned men of old were way ahead of what we "moderns" expected. However, the actual building of the pyramids was possible by the ancients themselves without help from spacemen.[23]

The claims of some ufologists are opposed to views of modern scientists such as archaeologists. We have said that Erich Von Daniken is not alone in suggesting levitation and other help from spacemen in the construction of various wonderful buildings of the past. There are many who write in that vein—such as Joseph Goodavage whose article, "Super Scientists from Nowhere,"[24] is interesting reading, though not convincing to this writer.

If the use of levitation in building could be proved —though it has not been—it would simply mean that activities now associated with spiritism were utilized in ancient times.

Dr. M. L. Jessup was one scientist who stated that the gigantic ruins in Central America were probably constructed with the help of men from outside this world, and that levitation techniques that are now unknown in scientific construction must have been used. This sort of argument is also used by some ufologists to explain how the Easter Island statues were built.[25]

Easter Island Gives Up Its Secret

Once again, however, it is not necessary to accept that levitation must have been used in these great constructions. To take one example, the writings of Thor Heyerdahl, especially *Aku-Aku*, make it clear that some of these things that supposedly could not be done without help from spacemen could have been undertaken by a small number of men with relatively simple techniques. Heyerdahl showed how the great stone statues could have been chiseled out of the volcanic stone, and that the statues themselves could be lifted by a process revealed and demonstrated to him by the mayor of Easter Island.[26] A few men used poles as levers while tiny stones were put beneath the selected statue, with larger stones being put under as the activity continued, until the statue was eventually standing on its feet. Then, with the help of 180 men, one of the statues was hauled eight miles across the plain at Easter Island, and then set up at the edge of the cliff. Today it looks out across the sea, as so many other statues do. Thor Heyerdahl did not need help from spacemen— nor levitation techniques either!

Analyzing Some "Explanations from Beyond"

Although he acknowledges he has no formal tertiary education, throughout his books Von Daniken speaks as though he is an authority in a number of disciplines—he represents himself as a virtual spokesman for archaeologists and historians, astronomers and engineers, cartographers and mathematicians, physicists and physicians, and theologians. He does not actually refer to Jesus Christ as being an astronaut, but he does make reference to the fact that some people would think of Jesus, Buddha, and Mohammed as astronauts. The front cover of the Australian edition highlighted the question, "Was God an Astronaut?"

He has sensed the human urge for an explanation "from beyond"—he has shown very real "psychological" discernment as well as commercial acumen. He reaches masses of people by his superficially exciting explanations, especially by his insistence on otherworldly visitors. Man is so created that he has a desire to find that which is beyond himself, a God or "gods" whose power is greater than that of man himself. For the man who rejects God as known to orthodox Christians, Von Daniken offers a plausible—but totally unconvincing—alternative. Something similar can be seen with the Israelites turning to Baal when they did not want to accept the holy standards of Yahweh.

In *Chariots of the Gods?* space travelers are conjectured to have wiped out human freaks, for, according to Erich Von Daniken, many experiments have taken place in cross-breeding between visitors from outer space and the inhabitants of earth.[27] Eventually, according to Von Daniken, extraterrestrial intelligent beings annihilated part of mankind and produced a new homo sapiens . . . yet they finally died out again.[28] It is very hard to follow! On this basis it is hard to understand how any of us are alive today—for modern man is referred to in anthropological circles as homo sapiens. Von Daniken seems confused at this point.

He even has talk of bodies awaking after an embalming process.[29] This of course is utter nonsense. Even if preservation of bodies in dry ice, or some other process, was one day found to be feasible so that bodies could be revitalized for repairs when medical and surgical knowledge had increased, that would be a totally different thing from what takes place with embalming. One has only to look carefully at the mummies in the Cairo Museum—or for that matter in other museums around the world—to realize that those bodies as such could never be revitalized. In the Mummy Room at the Cairo Museum many of the great Pharaohs of old lie, faces wizened like old leather, jugular veins protruding, and of course with their brains and intestines removed. Any human who submitted to this process because of some hope of bodily resurrection, a hope given by extraterrestrial visitors, would certainly be gullible.

Von Daniken refers to a "secret conference" at the U.S. National Radio Astronomy Observatory at Green Bank in West Virginia. The report of that supposedly secret conference is readily available to those interested—it is quoted in *Crash Go the Chariots*.[30] This is relevant to something else Von Daniken writes:

> There is no doubt about the existence of planets similar to earth—with a similar mixture of atmospheric gases, similar gravity, similar flora and possibly even similar fauna—

but that same "secret conference report" states:[31]

> Estimation of the average number of planets per system with environments suitable for the development of life, is a matter of pure guesswork.

Those Nazca Roads

The Nazca roads in Peru were apparently a great airfield, claims Von Daniken. However, the Reverend Donald Bond, a missionary at Nazca, told me that these lines are about four to six inches wide, and about half to one inch deep. He stated: "Von Daniken's suggestion is preposterous. Properly formed Inca roads run all through the Andes, but these lines have nothing to do with these roads. He stated it would be impossible to accept Von Daniken's theory if you saw the lines from the ground itself. Anyway, why 37-mile-long landing strips?[32] What was the braking system?

Actually astronomical observations show that many of the roads at Nazca point directly to the points at which particular stars rise. These people believed that the stars were inhabited by the gods, whom they sought to placate.

Von Daniken also made much of the bird and insect figures on these plains. In *Time* magazine of March 25, 1974, German scientist Maria Reiche explains that "the artists apparently worked out their designs in advance on small six-foot by six-foot plots still visible near many of the larger figures." She goes on to say they could break down each drawing into its component parts and "straight lines could be drawn by stretching a rope between two stakes." Curves were broken into smaller, linked arcs, and proof of her theory "lies in the fact that many drawings are pockmarked with stones and holes at points that are indeed centers for appropriate arcs."

Piri-Reis, the Turkish admiral, produced a map that was apparently "photographed" from a great height. The admiral himself acknowledged other maps from which he copied (not entirely accurately), and he also acknowledged his debt to a sailor who sailed with the famous "Colombo." Columbus had made his great voyage just a few years earlier.[33] The Piri-Reis maps were undoubtedly remarkably good for those times, but they are by no means the only maps from that period which have surprised cartographers by their advanced knowledge.

The picture in *Chariots of the Gods?* of a man with his space helmet on also has two serpents ready to "take off"—why were the serpents being taken on a space journey? And why doesn't the "astronaut" have shoes on? Did they not need their feet protected in those days? His mysterious weapons are the usual ones of the area where the drawing originated—there is clearly nothing to be taken seriously so far as spacemen are concerned here! Actually this is probably a picture of a ruler on a throne, making himself comfortable—probably while he was being carried by a team of slaves. This was a common practice, and rulers were carried in this way for many miles.

Many other points could be made, and of course Von Daniken gives a considerable amount of material that can be taken seriously—this is to be expected because he gives so very much, covering so many areas. The fact that Erich Von Daniken has written something does not automatically mean that it is therefore wrong, but the problem is that he has set himself up as the great authority, belittles scholarship, and challenges traditional beliefs in ways that are at least unfortunate. As we have already said, he has clouded the issue of UFOs. The question is a very real one, despite the wild hypotheses and conclusions of Erich Von Daniken.

In the 1980s the world has largely by-passed Von Daniken. His books still sell, but not in the huge numbers of the early 1970s. His hypotheses are not taken as seriously now, for so many of them have been shown to be unacceptable.

Many thinking people put the whole subject of UFOs in the same category. Perhaps we can learn by taking a tip from the skeptics. What if these are just hoaxes and hallucinations?

Chapter 8

Hoaxes and Hallucinations

Little green men from Mars . . . strange-eyed creatures without mouths . . . apelike monsters, twice as big as men . . . beautiful maidens and space journeys —these have all been subjects of much ridicule and laughter in the last twenty years. The setting is perfect for the hoaxers to cut loose, and they have done just that.

There are many strange stories about UFOs and their occupants which conceivably should be put under the category of hoaxes, but ufologists do not always regard them as such. There are a number of stories of UFOs hovering over an area, of cars being discharged from them, and then humanlike beings driving them off in different directions. There are other stories about men in black who impersonate FBI or intelligence agents, and even air force officers.[1] They are supposed to intimidate witnesses and demand negatives of photographs. Ufologists believe that thousands of witnesses are too frightened to reveal what they know because they have been intimidated by these men in black— sometimes they are not dressed in black, but that is a common pattern. Ufologists themselves are divided as to whether they are spacemen or really are government agents, disclaimed by the authorities because they do not want the true nature of their work to be revealed.

It stands to reason that some of the unexplained mysteries would be blamed on governments in that way. In 1947 U.S. Air Force statements admitted that no experimental craft like the UFOs was known, and that the air force was completely mystified. However, another U.S. Air Force statement issued on December 27, 1949, stated that the saucers were misinterpretations of various conventional objects, mild hysteria, meteorological phenomena, mental aberrations, or hoaxes. No doubt this was part of the truth, though certainly not all. Many investigations have eventually uncovered a hoax.[2]

One of the early "hoax" incidents, quoted by space writers, is that of A. H. Babcock. On November 26, 1896, he took a large box kite and launched it over Oakland in California. This led to a number of reports of an airship overhead.[3]

Thomas Edison and His Balloons

When he was young, even Thomas Edison played at games with balloons—at times he and his friends would fill big colored balloons with gas and send them off to float about for days.[4] At the time of the sightings in 1897 he suggested that possibly a game was being played by other tricksters.

It is common knowledge that many balloons have been sent up by students in deliberate attempts to find out the public reaction to these so-called saucers. However, a more serious test was made in Ottawa by a group under the direction of Wilbert B. Smith, the engineer in charge of the first Canadian saucer project.[5] A 500,000 candlepower aircraft flare was put inside an aluminum cone and sent up in a large weather balloon. It was deliberately let loose at a time when a night baseball game was on, and two drive-in theaters were operating. At 5,000 feet a delayed action fuse set off the flare, which then shone on the underneath side of the gas bag which had been sent aloft. The glowing effect was striking, and the experimenters expected there would be hundreds of calls, but there were none. It is possible that because the balloon was moving so slowly it did not catch the eye, whereas flying saucers move at tremendous speeds and are seen. However, it is also true that, in the main, people do not bother to look up at the sky except casually. In any case, some who saw it might have thought it was an airplane and not given it a second thought.

One problem has been that opinions among authorities have varied—some air force personnel felt that the public should be kept informed, while others believed that the only way out of this serious mysterious problem was to deny that it existed at all. Back in those years from 1947 through the early years of the 1950s, contradictions and changes of opinion were common, and official statements were confusing. Hoaxers did not help to reduce the confusion: in fact, they tended to ensure that the whole subject would be ridiculed.

A UFO "Load of Old Junk"

One of the most interesting hoaxes took place in September, 1969, when a "saucer" with a three-foot diameter was found beside the road at Shepton Mallet in Somerset, England. Surprised motorists heard it emitting a humming sound while its white dome was rotating and colored lights were flashing rhythmically. The police took it away and declared it was "a load of old junk" after they found leaking batteries inside. It was eventually returned to its owner, Edward Jaggers.[6]

The fact of hoaxes does not mean there are not genuine flying saucers. Some space journals report these hoaxes, for very often reputable people edit the journals, and in any case there is so much that is genuine that hoaxes are unnecessary as a way of establishing the case. One such exposure is in the January, 1970, volume of *Spacelink*. Two Danish men photographed a model flying saucer, then sent their photographs to a newspaper which gave the story front-page coverage. The next morning they announced that the whole thing was a hoax, and left the model at the office of the newspaper to prove their point.

Space journals do not automatically accept all photographs as genuine. In the April, 1971, volume of *Spacelink* there is a debunking of a supposed flying saucer photograph by a Japanese schoolboy. In the same volume there is another photograph showing up what some claimed was a UFO, in a picture taken by Bernardo Razquin in Mendoza, Argentina, in May, 1969. The reviewer does not suggest that this is a fake, but does say: "Although the photo has been published in other UFO magazines, we feel fairly sure that it is caused by a fault in the film rather than an actual UFO."

The point we are making is that those interested in UFOs and space vehicles include very many who are reputable persons of integrity, not anxious to deceive anybody, and quite prepared to acknowledge that something is not a UFO if they have reason to think otherwise.

Undoubtedly, there have been many hoaxes—that is not denied—but hoaxes add up to only a small percentage of UFO sightings. Despite the fact that there have been a number of hoaxes, and that some of the UFO reports seem totally incapable of belief, the similarities of supposed experiences around the world point to the reality of the majority of cases. As Dr. Hynek says:[7]

The reader will discover for himself that there is a very great similarity in accounts of occupant cases in reports from over the world. He will learn that they are similar not only in the description and the appearance of most humanoids but in their reported actions. He will find the occupants reportedly picking up samples of earth and rocks and carrying them aboard their craft, much as U.S. astronauts picked up moon rocks; he will find them seemingly exhibiting interest in human installations and vehicles; he will even find them making off with rabbits, dogs and fertilizers!

More Credible Witnesses

Dr. Hynek goes on to show that the contactees with these humanoid creatures are not pilots or air traffic control operators or radar operators, as with many of the reports of aerial phenomena. He indicates that these contactees are other types of reputable people, such as clergymen, policemen, electronics engineers, bank directors, medical doctors, and many others who are gainfully and creditably employed.

He also makes the relevant point that people with technical training and sophistication who have had humanoid contacts would be less likely to publicize their experience, because they would be especially wary of exposing themselves to ridicule. Despite this very real possibility, there are many reports of contacts from such people. Clearly, hoaxes are not the answer to the UFO phenomenon.

Sometimes these supposed visitors reported from space by reputable witnesses are huge apelike creatures on highways not far from New York; there are small men with slanted eyes and very thin lips; sometimes there are even people that are best described as mini-people—just a few inches in height.

Many who read such reports regard them as delusions or hallucinations on the part of those who "see" them, but there have been so many with credible witnesses that it is no longer convincing to smile, nod one's head and say, "Dream!" or "Hallucination!" Some of the experiences must be accepted as genuine.

At this point, this writer hesitates. To what extent is it desirable to identify with the way-out claims, journeys to and from distant planets—and so much more? Let it again be clearly stated that there *are* hallucinations, there *are* hoaxes, there *are* fantastic stories that are quite incredible except as personal experiences in the minds of the narrators. Such experiences are not limited to the late George Adamski—whose stories are "old hat" and are not utilized in this volume.

Various "wild" claims have been made. Undoubtedly some individuals capitalize on a gullible public, and at other times they themselves are suffering from hallucinations. Others again are deceived by "messages" which they might genuinely have received. Because of the overtones of the occult, it is not always possible to separate these into clear-cut categories.

There have been other "put-ons" that were not hoaxes in the usual sense of the word, but have produced somewhat similar, and lasting, reactions. One of the most alarming was Orson Welles's famous broadcast, "War of the Worlds," made on October 30, 1938. His startling suggestions as to the world being attacked by beings with intelligence greater than man's caused near-hysteria. Government authorities have been very much aware of this possibility, and have been anxious to avoid hysteria that could become national and even international if the wrong kind of announcement were made.

Psychological Problems

This leads to the various psychological and mental problems—*not* insanity—that can be involved. For instance, another "relative" to the hoax family is the falsification of memory. Where does this fit in an investigation of the UFO phenomenon? There is apparently much falsification of memory associated with contactees' stories, and this could well be attributed to the UFO occupants themselves. This falsification of memory is sometimes called confabulation.

This would mean that the contactees genuinely believed what they had been told. They could even believe that they had been taken to Mars, to Venus, or anywhere else, and that then their memories had been programmed so that they would insist on their stories, no matter how they were ridiculed or even tortured. At times there is undoubtedly much contradiction in UFO stories, especially as to the times involved, and what appear to be straight-out lies can be examples of this.

Over and over again these contactees are clearly not people who could invent the stories they tell, or continue with complicated hoaxes as they are interrogated by experts from various intelligence groups. Their experiences have been real, and the details correlate with those reported by others with whom they could have had no possible contact.

92

In such cases, if the messages from the contactees are false, or even if the "experiences" of the contactees are false, then the deception comes from those who gave the messages rather than from the contactees themselves. This is not to deny that there have been a number of hoaxes, and that not all of the messages are of the same type, nor that some of the stories have grown in the telling. We accept all that, and have yet become convinced that there is a pattern of consistency behind many stories.

The Ufonauts are Liars!

John Keel has the interesting comment that it is the ufonauts who are the liars, and not the contactees. He suggests they are deliberately lying and that this is part of the bewildering smokescreen so that their real origin, purpose, and motivation will not be known.[8]

In elaborating the sort of deception that has been undertaken, Keel goes on to say that people have undergone psychiatric and lie detector tests and passed supposedly came from, and have mentioned names such as Clarion, Maser, Orion, and Zombic. Keel them convincingly. They have told where the saucers points out that these are absurd place names, and in fact are not names of planets but of plants. He argues that whatever it is that the UFOs are up to, it is being done on a very large scale all over the earth, and that when contacts do take place, ridiculous false information is handed out. He claims that these beings hide behind the limited credulity of our scientists and our governments, and that part of the plan at present is to keep mankind confused and skeptical. The smokescreen—called "Hoax!"—is one of the ways by which the plan is successfully carried out.

We conclude that while many people have undoubtedly suffered from hallucinations with regard to UFOs, there are very many who have not so suffered and have actually seen them, and then have been contacted. It is also true that the person with highly developed psychic abilities is more likely to be contacted or to see these beings. Again, that does not limit the reality of what is seen: it is simply that some can see what others cannot see. This we discuss further in our chapter dealing with paraphysical phenomena.

Even apparent delusions of grandeur can at times be relevant in this study of UFOs, for a number of contactees have been carried away with their own new greatness since their "selection" by these mysterious visitors.

One man—among others—who was supposed to be the world's great savior was George King, a former attendant at the London office of an oil company, and before that a taxi driver for ten years—until ulcers forced him out. In 1954, George was drying his breakfast dishes in his apartment when a voice suddenly burned in his ear, "Prepare yourself. You are to become the voice of Interplanetary Parliament."[9]

George became quite famous by his practice of "charging" mountains—he insisted that while he went into a yogalike pose, space people actually used him as a "battery" so that mountains could be charged with spiritual power. George went on to produce a new "Bible" on tapes, taking five hours of playing time. It is good to note that the true Bible is still recognized by millions as the Word of God.

Prophetic Hoaxes

There are other more readily acceptable messages, touching on all sorts of details about the lives of the contactees—often giving information which was otherwise secret. At times the information concerned distant relatives, information at that time unknown to the contactee but which proved to be correct. In these ways confidence is gained, but we shall see that it appears to be part of a huge confidence trick.

Another supposed telepathic message was that the whole of the solar system was governed by a hierarchy, with an organization that ensured that specific groups watched over particular planetary systems. Another "message" stated that teleportation was used by the spacecraft as a means of creating a protective zone around the space vehicle, and that dials inside the vessel could be set for any particular place. When a button was pressed, it would produce a surge of time-space energy, and the vehicle and its crew would instantaneously materialize at the distant place to which the dial had been set.

These beings often claim great powers, as shown by the "message" to movie actor Stewart Whitman who starred in *Those Magnificent Men in Their Flying Machines*, and other well-known films. He was trapped in a twelfth floor suite of a New York hotel during the blackout of November, 1965. He looked out and saw two luminous disk objects, then heard a voice which stated that these beings were afraid of what was happening on earth—that earthlings might disrupt the balance of the universe. The "visitors" claimed that the blackout then in operation was only a small demonstration of their power, and that with almost no effort they could do much more—even to the extent of stopping the whole of our planet earth from functioning.[10]

Thus we conclude that some of the "messages" are interesting. However, even if we accept that messages have been given, that does not mean that the messages themselves are necessarily genuine information, for there clearly are hoaxes of a spiritual nature. We have already stated that relatively unimportant prophecies have been given and have then come to pass apparently as a setup for other greater prophecies with worldwide significance. These did not come to pass, but were believed in by many because of the earlier "fulfillments."

One famous prophecy was that New York City would subside into the ocean on July 2, 1967, and this date was accepted by UFO contactees and members of the "hippie" community in New York alike.[11] Obviously the prophecy was not fulfilled!

Literally thousands of mediums and UFO contactees

claim that they have received messages from "Mr. Ashtar" in recent years. "Ashtar" or "Ashtaroth" or "Asherah" was the name of a female deity of the Canaanites in biblical times. Archaeological evidence has added to the biblical picture of the evil practices of the Canaanite people, and it is not difficult to imagine the sort of conditioning that could be under way if there is a greatly increased hypnotism of evil influencing mankind in modern times. The opposition that was displayed in Bible times continues today. It was evil then, and it is just as evil in these modern times.

John Keel makes the point that the observed manifestations seem to be adapted to individual beliefs and mental attitudes: the information given conforms to the beliefs of those who are contacted. However, Keel also claims that a large part of the reported data is engineered and deliberately false. Therefore the witnesses are not the perpetrators of these hoaxes but are merely the victims. One apparent purpose of all this false data is to create confusion and diversion.[12]

The knowledge of these UFO occupants is great, and at times unexplainable. The details they can convey as to particular peoples, incidents, and even scientific knowledge are remarkable. Yet there are limitations to that knowledge, for we have seen that at times their "messages" prove to be quite erroneous.

Deuteronomy 18: 22 in the Bible says that the false prophet is shown to be such when his prophecies do not come to pass, and we have seen that many of the more important "prophecies" associated with these UFO occupants have not come to pass. These creatures aspire to the divine attribute of omniscience (all knowledge), but they are clearly limited in knowledge. Theirs is a "Mission Impossible."

The End of the World

One of the most glaring failures in the prophecies of Ashtar was that the world would end on December 21, 1954. North America would split in two, the Atlantic coast would sink into the sea, and the sea would also swallow up France, England, and Russia. Only a relatively small group would be rescued by spaceships. This was taken very seriously by Dr. Charles A. Laughead, a medical doctor on the staff of the Michigan State University in Lansing.[13] He had earlier received relatively minor prophecies which had come to pass, and as a result he took this prophecy to be true also. He made quite serious declarations to the press, and then with a group of friends gathered to await rescue, even leaving behind all metal objects, for they had been told to wear no metal.

Needless to say it was a spiritual hoax, and the world did not come to an end on December 21, 1954. This is interesting to put alongside the statement of Jesus Christ at Matthew 24: 36 that "no man knows the hour" when final events will take place.

Ashtar would not give up, and yet another date was set—December 24, 1967. Messages not only came from occupants of UFOs, but through Ouija boards all around the world—doomsday was set for December 24, 1967. When once again the crisis passed and doomsday had not happened, one of the most impressive of the contacts, named Knud Weiking, came up with an answer. Like Dr. Laughead, Knud Weiking had reported some earlier relatively minor prophecies which had come true, and he had taken a leading part in publicizing the December 24, 1967, date.[14] Now he declared that the watchers should have studied the Bible and they would have known that this was something of a trial run. He justified this from the New Testament story of the bridegroom who had not come when he was expected, and urged that a lesson should be learned—that the watchers should not be found without oil in their lamps, and should be ready for doomsday which would happen very soon.

One obvious conclusion can be drawn from the way these messages have been given through Ouija boards, at spiritists' séances, and through UFO entities: that there is a very real connection between them all. They are included in the spiritual "principalities and powers" against which the apostle Paul warned.

Yet a third man who had his reputation taken from him, and even became involved in antisocial activities, was Aladino Felix who took the name of Dino Kraspedon.[15] He made startling prophecies such as the assassinations of Martin Luther King and Senator Robert Kennedy. He accurately predicted various natural disasters, and then became involved with a wave of terrorist activities in Brazil in 1968. The ring was broken by government forces—and the terrorist leader turned out to be Aladino Felix, the so-called Dino Kraspedon. As with many others, he had been led along a path that ended in ruin.

There is an old saying that coming events cast their shadows. What is the purpose behind all this? Is there a pattern of evil—a pattern that can only be evil because of the sinister forces involved? Time will tell. In the meantime, let us be on guard, especially in the spiritual realm. UFO sightings can sometimes be attributed to hoaxes and hallucinations, but more often they are very real in the fullest sense. At times it becomes clear that spiritual forces are involved.

Hoaxes and hallucinations have not explained all sightings, and other solutions have necessarily been looked for. Various natural phenomena are put forward from time to time as the answer—often with definite justification. We shall consider some of these "natural phenomena" in our next chapter.

Chapter 9

On Mushrooms,
Mirages, and Myopia:
But Who Did Have Myopia?

Myopia is short-sightedness. We shall see that one of the most prominent UFO debunkers attributed myopia to Reverend William Gill, whose famous sighting in New Guinea has become recognized as one of the most important in modern times.[1] The vehicle was witnessed for some hours by a large number of mission personnel who signed a properly drawn-up statement.

Reverend Gill does not know of any myopic condition from which he suffers. However, before we analyze the way in which his sighting was "debunked" and blamed on myopia by Dr. Donald H. Menzel, astronomy professor at Harvard University, let us briefly survey some of the other "natural phenomena" explanations for UFOs. We shall find that the blame is laid on mushrooms and mirages, bell jars and birds, insects and ionized air, root rot and reflections of light, weather balloons and temperature inversions—and even cloud formations and marsh gas. The planet Venus is regularly "blamed" as a UFO sighting, and so also are the many satellites now in orbit around the earth. Undoubtedly many—not all—sightings are attributable to these phenomena.

Giant Mushrooms

One explanation given at times relates to giant mushrooms, especially the Argentina "hat" mushrooms, about thirty-five centimeters across. When they die, they disintegrate and combine with nitrogenous material in the soil to kill surrounding grass.[2] This possibly does explain some of the circles supposedly left by UFOs, and there are other "horticultural" explanations for some of those strangely burned areas. However, the fact that a small percentage can be explained in these ways does not rule out the possibility that at least some of the sites with strangely similar evidences bear the marks of UFO activity.

Sometimes such "natural" answers satisfy only those who give them. One case dates to September 4, 1969, when seemingly dehydrated radioactive scrub was found on a farm near Hamilton, in the northern island of New Zealand. The deep triangular depressions often associated with reported UFO landings were found, and the surrounding vegetation was perfectly healthy. The farmer said there had been no weed spraying or scrub blight in that area. A horticultural consultant went on record as stating, "No earth-bound source of energy could account for the circle, but government nuclear scientists had a very simple answer: 'root rot and blight.' "[3] That official answer certainly did not satisfy all parties.

A similar explanation that has become famous in UFO writings is the "swamp-gas" theory first put out by Dr. J. Allen Hynek. It is interesting that he eventually "changed sides" and came out with the outstanding volume referred to a number of times in this survey.

The "swamp-gas" theory related to a UFO sighting near Ann Arbor, Michigan, in March, 1966. This clear sighting by dozens of witnesses was attributed to marsh gas (methane) resulting from organic decomposition, which was then ignited by combustion. Dr. Hynek later stated that there was little scientific fact to support this theory, and he had intended it only as a possible explanation.[4] It happened to "catch on," to his own subsequent embarrassment, because of unfair cartoons and misrepresentations.

The writer Gerald Herd, in *Is Another World*

Watching?, had yet another way-out theory—that we were being investigated by a breed of superinsects, humanlike in their intellectual capacities but not using audible speech. To support this argument, a number of space writers have pointed out something to which we have already referred—that many animals hear things that have a higher frequency than we humans can hear, and that there could also be differences of frequency, etc., associated with other races from outside our planetary system.

Yet another natural phenomenon theory was put forward by two engineers in Chicago—that the saucers could be explained as a side effect from atomic bomb tests that had taken place in Nevada. According to this theory the saucers were nothing more than pockets of ionized air. However, this had already been thoroughly investigated and discounted. It did not explain the various problems such as the maneuverability of those strange vehicles in the sky.

Another theory was associated with "the bell-jar experiment" by which miniature "saucer lights" could be produced. However, experts pointed out that although this phenomenon could be produced in a laboratory, it was not known to be duplicated in nature. They also made the point that flying saucer lights showed strong evidence of being navigated, with reversals, fantastically sharp turns, etc., in a way that was simply not associated with natural phenomena and the ionosphere. This fact of maneuvering made the explanations associated with natural phenomena, storms, birds, etc., very difficult to accept. So-called ground clutter was well known to radar technicians, and experts have claimed that it was not an explanation for the blips constantly seen on first-class radar screens. On some occasions those blips were actually pinpointed by no less than three reputable radar stations, with lights being seen simultaneously from a number of points, both on the ground and in aircraft.

Such unwelcome reports have continued persistently through the 1970s and 1980s.

Birds in the Sunlight

It seems possible that some people have mistaken the underneath of birds shining against the sunlight for UFOs. Soon after the frightening experiences over Washington in 1952, one of the explanations officially given in the USA to explain blips on radar was that birds also could show up on radar. However, at that time to many people this seemed to be an attempt to defuse the whole issue, as also were statements suggesting that the saucers were "something" that had unlimited power but no mass. This seemed close to the idea that the saucers were simply mass hallucinations—for to most people "no mass" meant that there was nothing physically solid about the saucers. However, only a month later air force intelligence frankly admitted that even Dr. Menzel's temperature inversion theory could not explain the sightings over Washington.

This temperature inversion theory should be explained. Although air gets colder with higher altitudes, it is possible for there to be a layer of warm air higher than the cold air. Light rays are refracted (bent) as they pass from cold air to warm air, and this is what causes mirages in deserts, or on heated roads where nonexistent pools of water can be "seen" ahead. Dr. Menzel, professor of astronomy at Harvard University, claimed that the same principle applied to many UFOs picked up on radar screens—deflected radar beams had been re-reflected because of the inversion layer, and so had shown up as blips on radar screens. Reflections of cars, trains, or other fast-moving objects (and even turbulence in the inversion layer) could give the impression of fantastic speeds and maneuverability.[5]

This reversal of their public stand indicated that the phenomenon was taken seriously by U.S. government authorities: since the Washington sightings, other incidents had forced a revision of official opinion.

This reversal of policy was made even clearer by a report ordered to be released by U.S. Major-General

John A. Samford. It related to two cases which seemingly made it forever clear that saucers were solid objects, at least at the time they were sighted. The story is fully recounted by Donald Keyhoe. The witnesses included a number of aircraft personnel who observed the saucers, together with ground tracking, sightings by civilians, and even camera shots. An object that could keep just ahead of pursuing aircraft, that would appear simultaneously and in the same position according to radar screens on the ground and in the air, that could move against the wind, and could be photographed, was not explainable by the temperature inversion theory nor by any other known explanation involving natural phenomena. The stories were released to Keyhoe with an insert from the air defense command to the effect that no orders had been issued for fighter units to fire on unidentified aerial phenomena.[6]

This report indicated that in a matter of a few weeks the United States Air Force had come to realize that they must begin to take the public into its confidence, and the government had realized that to antagonize the saucer occupants could be an extremely foolhardy practice. However, the mystery itself remained unsolved.

The Temperature Inversion Theory

We have referred to the temperature inversion theory, and Professor Donald Menzel of Harvard is especially linked with this theory. In the early 1950s this man of science did much to show that many of the so-called flying saucers should be attributed to natural phenomena.

Donald Keyhoe put a whole series of questions about Dr. Menzel's theories to "Project Blue Book," and in the offical answer it was acknowledged that prominent scientists had analyzed Menzel's claims and that his answers had not always been accepted. Keyhoe tells of hundreds of fighters having been "scrambled" to intercept UFOs in a two-year-period—there had been blips from these strange machines on many radar screens, both in the United States and at foreign bases. For many of the so-called sightings Menzel had very easy "solutions," even for some sightings that were quite unexplained by air technical intelligence.[7]

One such case was that of Captain Thomas Mantell, who died when his fighter plane crashed during the chase of a flying saucer. Thousands of people in Kentucky witnessed that same unidentified object, including the commanding officer and several pilots and operators of the control tower at Godman Field. Dr. Menzel's explanation seemed far too simple—that Mantell had been lured to his death by a "sun dog," which is the name for a glowing mock sun that is actually caused by the sun shining on ice crystals forming in cirrus clouds. This implied that the other witnesses were just as deluded in their belief as Mantell himself had been.

Another typical "solution" which Menzel put forward related to a sighting in 1948 by pilots of Eastern Air Lines. This strange craft was encountered near Montgomery in Alabama, and it was also seen over Macon in Georgia. According to Menzel the witnesses were all misled by a mirage, again caused by layers of hot and cold air. We have seen that this explanation was put forward to explain many of the so-called sightings, and probably it is a sufficient answer for some of them. However, such an answer, which would possibly be acceptable when only one person sighted the particular "mirage," would not be acceptable when the sightings were spread over a large area, confirmed on radar, and in other ways shown to be "solid" objects.

Another of Menzel's "explanations" concerned a fighter pilot who chased a maneuvering light over Fargo in South Dakota—he had seen a light reflection that was caused by a whirlpool of air over the fighter's wing tip. Keyhoe put questions to "Project Blue Book" about Menzel's "sun dog" explanation, the Eastern Air Lines sighting, and the supposed light reflection over Fargo in South Dakota. In each case the answer was that "Project Blue Book" did not accept Dr. Menzel's explanations in these cases.

Ufologists have at times pointed out that those who give these debunking answers sometimes put the United States Air Force in a tight corner, in that they are forced to say what the saucers are *not*. At a time when there was very real fear of the possibility of an invasion from outer space, this was considered a real risk, not in the best interests of national security.

Reports from Pilots

During those years of the early 1950s the U.S. Air Force had the serious problem that reports kept coming in, indicating the reality of saucers, but it seemed the only answer was that they came from outer space. Hundreds of civilian pilots reported seeing them, and intelligence even had special UFO report forms. Radar operators were asked to give careful reports, and these were followed by interrogation and investigation. Despite all this, because of the seeming danger to security, representatives of the government still did their best in public to brush off the possibility of saucers being solid objects. Over a period, the public stand was not consistent, and that is not surprising. This "new" phenomena represented a great problem, and contrasting opposing beliefs as to the best course of action were sincerely held by high officials.

The explanation that they were natural phenomena was totally unacceptable to many airline pilots. They told stories of disks that kept their distance, but were able to maneuver whenever the attempt was made either to close in on them or to climb away. Many pilots came to realize they would be helpless if whoever controlled the so-called space vehicles decided to attack. Air force pilots were scrambled many times to chase UFOs, and yet in public there were denials that there were any such things. Many reports showed that aircraft radar, ground radar, visual sighting from the aircraft, and even visual sighting from the ground, confirmed the reality of the "thing"—that it was not some atmospheric phenomenon, nor an inversion effect in the clouds, nor a reflection, nor a malfunction of a radar set. The coinciding factors as to the sightings, with plottings leading from differing points to the same precise spot where the UFO was, were such that it could not be a mere hallucination or a delusion. These things were real. Civilian and air force pilots alike had no doubt on that score.

They also had no doubt that they could not be controlled by earth beings, for the way they turned at right angles, and even completely reversed their direction in a flash of time, was such that no human being could take all the "Gs" that were involved. (One "G" is the normal pull of gravity on an earthling.) There was some intelligence in control of those craft, for over and over again their maneuverings made it clear that they were so controlled. It was recognized that it might be remote control, including some sort of television or similar observation.

Despite the fact that UFOs could not be explained in human terms, many pilots and others who had had firsthand experience with them made a joke out of the whole business, because so many people ridiculed those who saw these things. They knew too that others had the impression that a person was not normal if he was scared by "nonexistent" saucers. Others still thought they were a secret United States weapon.

Dr. Menzel was so satisfied that he had the explanation that in one of his articles he even assured the public that the whole problem of flying saucers would disappear when the current heat spell had ended.[8] In fairness it should be stated that Dr. Menzel became more cautious with his explanations in later years.

With all due respect to a reputable scientist such as Dr. Menzel, far too much has been put down to "natural phenomena." In our chapter on "The Credibility of the Witnesses," we showed how Dr. J. Allen Hynek, chairman of the Department of Astronomy at Northwestern University, came around from being an amused skeptic to one who argued that the UFO phenomenon must be thoroughly investigated scientifically. He indicated that the natural phenomenon answer was not always convincing.

The New Guinea Episode

As an appendix to his book, Dr. Hynek gives an analysis by Dr. Menzel of the sighting by Reverend William Gill and others in New Guinea—we have already referred to this famous case of a UFO sighting. Dr. Menzel does his best to debunk Mr. Gill's experience and makes seemingly unjustified assumptions such as:[9]

> We are first to assume that Father Gill and Stephen Gill Moi [teacher] both suffer from appreciable myopia and they were not wearing spectacles during the sighting. They probaby had appreciable stigmatism [sic] as well, so that the image of Venus was large and definitely elongated.

Dr. Menzel goes on to suggest that the men waving was an optical illusion, and that as the mission personnel were conditioned to miracles, this conditioning was part of the explanation. He suggests that the New Guinea personnel "would not have been too surprised because after all, they looked upon Father Gill as a holy man." Thus, in this report (dated December 20, 1967) Dr. Menzel wrote off Reverend Gill's sighting to his own satisfaction, and states that he shall henceforth consider the Father Gill case as solved.

However, in this same survey, Dr. Menzel says, "I should be very much interested to know whether or not Father Gill wears glasses, what his correction is, and finally whether he was wearing them on that evening." This is a remarkable statement, for the whole conclusion is based on Father Gill's "myopia," and the analysis shows that Dr. Menzel does not even know whether or not Father Gill wears glasses! Dr. Hynek has an excellent brief summary on the point. He states:[10]

> The self-styled "arch enemy of UFOs," Dr. Donald Menzel, of Harvard, has taken a characteristic opposite

view. In his *analysis of the Papua-Father Gill case* . . .
he dismisses the entire case as a sighting of Venus under
the hypothesis that Reverend Gill was not wearing his
glasses at the time. Unfortunately he neglected to ascer-
tain the following: The UFO at times was seen under
cloud cover; Venus was pointed out separately by Gill;
and Reverend Gill was wearing properly corrected glasses
at the time.

Reverend William Gill and this author have become
personal friends, and we have discussed Dr. Menzel's
analysis, together with the comments of Dr. Hynek.
Mr. Gill adopts a very gracious attitude toward critics
such as Dr. Menzel, even though these conclusions in
writing, widely publicized, are surprisingly far from the
facts, especially when one remembers that this analysis
is put out by a man of undoubted scientific achievement.

A Talk with Reverend William Gill

It is clear that Dr. Donald Menzel is—to repeat—
what he has himself called the "arch enemy of UFOs."
His analysis of the widely publicized sighting by Father
Gill is a disturbing document. Let it be repeated that
Dr. Menzel is a professor of astronomy at Harvard, one
of the top universities in the United States and, indeed,
in the whole world. It was therefore virtually incredible
to read through his analysis of Reverend Gill's sighting:
even before discussing that analysis with Reverend Gill
himself, it was clear that here was a nonscientific approach in a supposedly scientific analysis of an observed phenomenon.

In that analysis, reported as an appendix to Dr. Hynek's book, *The UFO Experience—a Scientific Inquiry,* Dr. Menzel makes surprising statements. He
says that Reverend Gill and the mission group do not
refer to Venus, and he finds it "unconvincing" that "a
number of the Mission boys (and girls) seemed to cor-
roborate the sighting." A number of assumptions follow. We have already quoted Dr. Menzel as assuming

that Reverend Gill and Stephen Moi probably suffered appreciably from both myopia and astigmatism. He then says:[11]

> Something of this sort is necessary to account for the difference in appearance of the UFO as reported by the two individuals ... Could these gasps have been of incredulity because of the inability to see what Father Gill was reporting?

Then, according to Dr. Menzel, "In a mission of this sort, the natives must have been conditioned to miracles and the like." A little further on he states, "Father Gill simply assumed that the other people were seeing what he saw"; then, "Although a great many 'witnesses' signed the report, I doubt very much that they knew what they were signing or why." He even suggests that these local people "would certainly have been mystified as to why their great leader was seeing something that was invisible to them"—however, according to Dr. Menzel, "they would not have been too surprised because after all, they looked upon Father Gill as a holy man."

Dr. Menzel makes the observation in passing that many people in this world need glasses and fail to wear them, and then he immediately makes the further observation, "I should be very much interested to know whether or not Father Gill wears glasses, what his correction is, and finally, whether he was wearing them on that evening." On the basis of these observations, Dr. Menzel has explained the New Guinea sighting to his own satisfaction, and states, "I shall henceforth consider the Father Gill case as solved."

Outlandish Statement

So outlandish did these statements seem—and amazing, coming from a man of very high scientific qualifications—that I decided to go over them with Mr. Gill. We made it a trio—we invited Kevin Arnett, a highly reputed radio announcer with the Australian Broadcasting Commission. Reverend Gill has not bothered to answer Dr. Menzel's criticisms, for he does not feel that he himself has a special brief to defend UFO sightings, or for that matter to attack critics such as Dr. Menzel. Reverend Gill is a very gracious man, of kindly disposition, very much more inclined to justify his opponents than to condemn them out of hand. In fact, as we discussed the analysis, he "bent over backwards" to show that Dr. Menzel was personally sincere in his hypotheses and conclusions. Let it therefore be again stressed that this analysis of Dr. Menzel's analysis is not Reverend Gill's idea—he has not set out to defend himself, and he has no desire to belittle the scholarship of Dr. Menzel. At the same time, it should also be stated that Mr. Gill has given permission for me to write in this way. He has no objection to the record being set straight where there have been misconceptions or misunderstandings.

First let us look at Dr. Menzel's statement as to "a great many uneducated natives of Papua" seeing these remarkable objects. These were not "uneducated natives": Reverend Gill is himself an educator, and these people were not superstitious beings who knew nothing of "civilization" and modern education. Their native language is Wedau, but after Grade 3 level—at that time (several years ago) this would mean from about nine to eleven years of age—their education was in English. They were certainly not "uneducated natives."

Dr. Menzel suggests that none of the sightings by Reverend Gill and the Mission group referred to the planet Venus, but Reverend Gill very clearly mentions in the widely circulated report of his sighting that he saw the planet Venus as well as the UFO. He himself suggested a "let-out" for Dr. Menzel at this point—that he had probably read one of the many abbreviated versions of this famous sighting. If Dr. Menzel had seen the full report he surely would not have said that Venus had not been referred to. His statement at this point is simply not according to the facts.

On Wearing Glasses

I asked Reverend Gill if he could read without his glasses, and then I opened a book at random—set in this type size—and asked him to read a paragraph. As Kevin Arnett and I listened, it was very obvious that Mr. Gill had no problem whatever, reading fluently, without hesitation. I questioned Mr. Gill about his wearing of glasses, and he says that basically they had been prescribed for when he was driving. At no time had he ever previously heard any suggestion that he himself suffered from myopia, which is one of the basic assumptions of Dr. Menzel. As I asked him about his habit with spectacles, he told me that he invariably puts his glasses on as soon as he goes outside—this is his normal way of life, and his glasses were not broken or lost at the time of the sighting. To him the fact of wearing glasses outside would be in the same category as wearing shoes or sandals. He would only remember not having them on if they had been lost or broken, and he is quite definite that that was not the case.

Dr. Menzel suggests that the teacher Stephen Gill Moi also suffered from appreciable myopia, and probably had appreciable astigmatism as well. Reverend Gill made the point to me that Stephen Moi certainly did not wear glasses at any time—he simply did not have them—and that his eyesight was obviously of a very high standard. He told how at times Mr. Moi would point out to sea and describe a ship on the horizon, before Mr. Gill himself had seen it. Clearly, Dr. Menzel's theory about glasses and eye defects does not stand up to investigation. Stephen Moi has never had problems with recognizing children, or using the blackboard—and he simply did not own glasses.

Dr. Menzel suggested that his theory about their eye problems was necessary because "something of this sort is necessary to account for the difference in appearance of the UFO as reported by the two individuals. Father

Gill had the long axis of the vehicle horizontal; Stephen had it more nearly vertical."

Mr. Gill could not understand this—he made the point that he and Stephen Moi were in fact standing together, and he wondered if Dr. Menzel was confusing two different sightings. As one goes back to the reports of the sightings given by Reverend Gill, it turns out that Stephen Moi reported seeing UFOs before Mr. Gill did. Mr. Gill actually wrote a letter to a colleague in which he told of Stephen Moi's supposed sighting of a UFO, and he signed himself as "Doubting William." However, he wrote with great surprise a short time later to that same colleague, telling that now he, with all these other witnesses, including Stephen Moi, had had this further experience. Now "Doubting William" signed himself as "Convinced Bill."

One relevant point is that, instead of all these people seeing the object because "their great leader" Reverend Gill did, the situation was just the opposite. One of their own number saw UFOs before Reverend Gill himself ever saw it. Talk about natives being conditioned to miracles, as in Dr. Menzel's analysis, simply does not make sense. Reverend Gill's own earlier skepticism does not suggest he was personally "conditioned to miracles."

No Role-Playing in a New Guinea Village

As to the statement that "Father Gill simply assumed that the other people were seeing what he saw," Mr. Gill made the point that he himself knows the Wedau language thoroughly—he was entirely conversant with these people who were with him, people with whom he had lived in the closed circle of a New Guinea village for some eight years. He said there was no assumption about what was being seen, and the people certainly would not have professed to see something just to please him, or to fit into his beliefs. In a small village, strengths and weaknesses are known, and if there were doubts about these strange happenings, undoubtedly they would have been expressed: there is no possibility of "role-playing." The whole incident was discussed widely, and in any case there were enough factions in the village to ensure that if the incident had been a fabrication, the deceivers would have been exposed. Mr. Gill made the point that a number of those who were there and had actually witnessed the sighting later went into the towns and became very good leaders. Their record of the observation has not been discredited, nor have they retracted it.

The report itself was in English, and there were detailed sketches that accompanied it. These were a bilingual people, and they were competent in the English language. The signatures have been reproduced in various volumes, and they also are written in English. Mr. Gill was emphatic that these were not illiterate people, and that they thoroughly understood what it was they were signing, despite Dr. Menzel's statement, "I doubt very much if they knew what they were signing and why."

Reverend Gill mentioned that Dr. Hynek had recently visited the area where the incident took place, and had interviewed some of those involved. A schoolteacher named Ananias had put down his impressions on tape, and had again described many of the significant features of this exciting episode that had taken place about fourteen years previously. Despite the time lapse, significant points were still clearly remembered. Ananias was somewhat hazy about exact locations and times, but the significant points were still reported in detail.

Dr. Menzel also refers to Mr. Gill as these people's "great leader," and states that they looked upon him "as a holy man." Mr. Gill strongly emphasized that they were not submissive or subservient, and he elaborated this as a real virtue. He stressed that in the subsequent years many of them have become capable leaders in the towns.

Thus it is clear that Dr. Menzel's declaration that "I shall henceforth consider the Father Gill case as solved" is not acceptable to others who view the facts dispassionately.

One point that worried me was that if this particular analysis is so suspect, what about so many others that have been explained to the satisfaction of Dr. Menzel? Because of his status, his explanations would satisfy many people who would take the understandable attitude that here was a top man of science who had investigated thoroughly and rejected the UFO phenomena as without substantial foundation. He himself says at the end of his analysis of the Reverend Gill's sighting, "Moreover, I feel that the same phenomena are responsible for some of the more spectacular, unsolved cases in the air force files." One comes away unconvinced by Dr. Menzel's logic.

However, in fairness to Dr. Menzel, it should be stated that many of his explanations do make sense, as the article "Flying Saucers Do Not Exist" makes abundantly clear.[12]

An ABC Reporter Comments

I asked Reverend Gill a number of leading questions. One was, "Have you ever again seen a UFO?" and his answer was "No." He and his children have watched satellites crossing the sky, as many of us have, and in the mountainous areas of New Guinea he has seen fireballs on three occasions—and fully accepted that this was simply a natural phenomenon. Kevin Arnett interrupted with a chuckle to mention that he and Reverend Gill had stood together one night and watched a moving object in the sky—at first they had actually thought it might be a UFO, but then as they saw its steady progress across the sky they realized that it was a satellite. Clearly these were not men who were anxious to see UFOs behind every cloud, but they had become convinced by the evidence.

Kevin Arnett addresses meetings regularly on the subject of UFOs, and in our discussion at this time he mentioned that there is hardly a meeting—and he has addressed a great number—at which there is not someone who comes to him afterward and says something like this: "Look, I have never told anybody because I don't want to be laughed at—I haven't even told my relatives because they would not believe me. But I have actually seen a UFO . . . ," and then follows a description of what took place.

Kevin then told of one of his most recent meetings, within the previous few days, at which five airline pilots had been present—though he had not known they would be. Of those five pilots who regularly fly across Australian skies, three had actually seen UFOs, and all of them knew of other pilots who had seen them. Australian pilots are briefed from time to time as to where UFOs are most often seen. It is no longer a matter of amusement to pilots—they know that the UFO phenomenon is a matter of reality, though they do not necessarily say they know the answer to the problem.

I asked Reverend Gill what he thought about Erich Von Daniken's writings, especially *Chariots of the Gods?*. His answer was that he personally was pleased in some ways that this book had received the publicity it did, because it had provided a tremendous stimulus so that people were now very much more ready to take an interest in ancient history, archaeology, and religion. He stated he had found that young people were more stimulated through these writings than through any other writings spread over his own career as a teacher. As the chaplain in a grammar school he finds that young people bring the subject up regularly in about the second year of their high school education. He made the point that the interest stretches across ability ranges, and is not limited either to those who are especially bright or to those who are especially dull. Young people are taking an interest in ancient history where previously it was hard to get them to take any interest, even in something as old as World War II.

Reverend Gill then went on: "However, I question many of Von Daniken's hypotheses. He appears to portray a hypothesis as just that, but in fact, in the way he presents it, those hypotheses are actually leading questions to which the reader is expected to say yes. In that I quite definitely disagree with him."

As one talks with Reverend Gill, there is a deep impression that the man is utterly sincere. The unprejudiced investigator would come away satisfied that this man undoubtedly saw a UFO.

William Booth Gill does not, and did not, suffer from myopia. In a sense, many who have taken so long to become convinced have been the ones who *did* suffer from a form of "mental myopia.". It is time to put those glasses on!

We have referred to airline pilots acknowledging they have seen UFOs in the Australian skies. Since the first edition of this book was printed I have talked to many reputable people, not only in the airline business but in upper echelons of the United States Air Force as well. One particular interview with an Air Force Colonel was especially enlightening, for he was a high official with access to top secret documents.

He asked me not to reveal his name or office, and for many that would immediately throw doubt on his credibility. It does not really. It simply means that he had no authority to reveal what he personally knew.

His name and office no longer matter. The vast amount of material now released from official files amply supports all he told me. The secrets of the 1970s are common knowledge in the late 1980s.

The world faces terror in the skies. It is a stark reality.

Chapter 10

A Hollow Earth?
A Parallel World?
Another Planet?

If we accept that UFOs are a "real" phenomenon, it is then relevant to ask, "Where do they come from?" Our own conclusion will be dealt with in a later chapter, but first let us glance at several other suggestions.

Some we merely mention—neither to disparage nor to endorse, but simply to state that there are such theories. They include time machine concepts, with visitors who are actually our own descendants returning to examine us. Others suggest a reverse procedure—our forefathers coming ahead through time. Allied to these are suggestions of television-like projections from either past or future. Yet others suggest that these manifestations are really the way in which the suppressed mind of the masses demonstrates its united power over matter.

None of these has convinced this writer, but each has adherents. We stress that we recount the stories and theories: we do not necessarily accept them at face value.

A Hollow Earth Inside Our Earth?

Another theory is that there is a hollow earth within our own.[1] This hollow earth theory is not new, having been written about for at least a century. There are stories in UFO literature of Scandinavian fishermen who are supposed to have accidentally sailed through a great hole at the North Pole, and to have spent some time living in the company of the gentle giants who inhabited a beautiful land inside the earth.

An old man named Olaf Jansen told the story on his deathbed of how he and his father had entered the inside of the earth through a hollow opening at the North Pole, in a small fishing boat. He claimed that they had spent two years among these giant people, and that they had an amazingly advanced technology. They were supposed to live from 400 to 800 years of age, and to be twelve feet and more in height. They operated spacecraft by utilizing electromagnetism which they drew from the atmosphere, and had remarkably developed the functioning of their mental capacities. According to space writers, Olaf's father was killed when an iceberg struck their fishing vessel as they were returning from this land of the inner earth, and Olaf himself was locked up as insane when he tried to convince people of his fantastic voyage.

There was even a sun inside the hollow earth but it seemed to be smoky, and the giants who inhabited the land referred to it as "The Smoky God." This is the basis of the record by Willis George Emmerson who claimed to have befriended Olaf Jansen before he died: he had been bequeathed the old man's manuscripts and maps. Emmerson's record was published as *The Smoky God* in 1908, and it was reprinted in 1965.

Many who are not identified with ufology still champion this theory of a hollow earth civilization, and a surprisingly large number of people have some belief in it. Even Hitler is supposed to have believed in it, and to have sent an expedition in April, 1942, to make a thorough investigation. The argument is that he had a fanatic belief that he himself was the one who should work in close cooperation with these supermen so that a new race of demigods could be created.

There are many ancient legends which deal with people who inhabited a subterranean world—sometimes they are giants, sometimes demigods, and sometimes beings who are actively hostile toward the inhabitants of the earth. Among these latter are the malformed creatures called deros, supposedly subhuman robot types who not only occupy the hollow earth itself but actually live beneath cities all over the world. Often they are said to have come from an original home called Lemuria, and to have as their main occupation the persecution of human beings who lived above them. Many space writers believe in them, and seriously report all sorts of contacts made by the deros with normal human beings.

A Message from Mr. Ashtar!

There are other supposed contacts and messages that touch on this concept of a hollow earth. Not all are readily acceptable—as with the case of Allen Noonan. He claims that one day while working for his company on an outdoor billboard he was suddenly transported in astral form to another place. He found himself in the midst of a group of elders sitting around a glowing throne. A great voice boomed out, "Will you agree to be the savior of the world?"[2] Noonan told all sorts of strange stories about his contacts with space visitors, and alleged visits to planets such as Venus. He passed on many telepathic messages, these again coming from Ashtar, to whom we have already referred and who is referred to so often by UFO contacts. In one of his interviews Allen Noonan made this statement:[3]

> The space command flies in and out of the earth. The earth is hollow and the Higher Command, the Galactic Command, already has bases inside the earth. There are great openings at each pole of the earth, and what we call the northern lights is only the Great Central Sun shining out of these openings. Many people coming from the Polar regions have reported seeing flying saucers there which disappeared into the ocean.

Ashtar has supposedly appointed others to be the great deliverer for this space age, some of them becoming fanatics for their new cause. One of them,[4] "Dino Kraspedon" to whom we have already referred, even wrote a supposedly new "Bible" before he became a terrorist in Brazil.

Hundreds of UFOs seem to come from the Arctic regions to the north, and there have also been great arcs of sightings across Norway, Sweden, and Finland. Many other reports have come from northern Greenland, with radar as well as visual sightings involved. There have been hundreds of observed flights in these areas, and many "hollow earth" theorists are convinced that flying saucers are coming out of a hole somewhere near the North Pole. It should, however, be stated that some other space writers have a different theory—that UFOs come in from outer space at the polar regions to avoid the intense radiation belts that are concentrated above the earth at the temperate zones.

What Did Admiral Byrd See?

A number of space writers quote Admiral Byrd as having seen lakes, forests, and mountains when he flew over the North Pole in 1947, and they state that Admiral Byrd himself said he flew beyond the North Pole, not over it.[4] They suggest that at the poles there are unknown and very extensive land areas that are not inhabitable, but are actually the size of large continents.

When asked how it is that airline pilots do not report this mysterious land, the answer given is that they do not actually fly directly over the North Pole but around it. Ufologists then argue that this is nothing to do with magnetic interference, compasses, etc., but that if pilots flew over the North Pole itself they would in fact fly inside the hollow earth.

Not only the North Pole, but the South Pole too is included in this hollow earth theory, with a great opening at the South Pole as well as at the North Pole.

A typical expression of this view is in *The Allende Letters*, by Brad Steiger and Joan Whritenow:[5]

Lt. Cdr. David Bungar was at the controls of a large U.S. Navy transport in February, 1947, when he discovered "Bungar's Oasis" in Antarctica. About the time that Admiral Byrd was making his discovery of "the land beyond the Pole," Bungar and his crew were flying inland from the Shackleton Ice Shelf near Queen Mary Coast of Wilks Land. Here Bungar discovered a series of warm water lakes—a condition which Bungar tested by landing his seaplane on one—surrounded on two sides by great ice walls 100 feet high and on the other two sides by gradual slopes. Had the lakes been created by warm winds blowing from the earth's interior?

In *The Hollow Earth*, Bernard tells of a photograph published in 1960 in the Toronto, Canada, *Globe and Mail* which shows a beautiful valley with lush, green hills. An aviator claimed that the picture had been taken from his airplane as he flew "beyond the North Pole."

Others who argue that there is an entrance through the poles refer to strange facts such as the musk ox migrating to the north in winter. They point out that the farther north one goes, the warmer it gets, with a north wind bringing relatively warm weather near the North Pole, and coniferous trees drifting ashore in that area where there are supposed to be no trees.

Some space writers see a parallel between the Scandinavian legend of the paradise to the north, known as "Ultima Thule," and this little-known paradise inside the earth itself. They even speak of icebergs having within them quantities of sand and earth, and of human bodies recovered in the Antarctic, seemingly coming from nowhere. They also point out that huge quantities of fresh water are required for icebergs, and that this could not come from the salt water sea—they suggest it comes from freshwater rivers inside the earth. Other more orthodox writers recognize that huge quantities of water are locked up at the poles.

This writer remains unconvinced that there are beings who inhabit a hollow earth inside our own earth, and believes there are other answers to the occasional factors of interest which these theorists put forward.

Some of the answers involve the happenings of the last great ice age which probably ended only a few thousand years ago. A number of problems, such as that of the tropical flora found beneath the Antarctic ice cap, could possibly be explained by a sudden tilt of the earth's axis, causing very great climatic changes in prehistoric times.

A Parallel World?

Yet another theory is that there is a world parallel to our own world, in a different dimension, as it were. The argument is that if we were set free from gravity and its effects, we could possibly move from the universe we know into a "new" universe in the same space continuum. If there is what is scientifically called antimatter, as opposed to matter, that antimatter might be unaffected by the earth's gravitational pull. Fantastic speeds of UFOs could thus be explained.

Theoretically, so some physicists hold, it would be possible for several such systems to coexist as long as each had a gravitational system that was not attracted to any of the others. According to this theory, gravity is governed by a curvature of space, and so other universes could coexist if they in turn were governed by different spatial curvatures. Dr. Barry H. Downing is one who discusses this in some detail. He states, "Our own space may be curved, either in a negative or positive direction or it may have a zero curvature."[6] He goes on to refer to "Jordan's Curve Theorem," and further states:[7]

This idea seems to imply that if our universe is similar to a closed curve, then there might be an "inside" and an "outside" universe coexisting *in the same space* with our own universe. We are led to ask the question: Would it be possible for the universes of different spatial curvatures to coexist in the same space? Could you move from one universe to another provided you understood the spatial curvature, or gravitational formula for each space?

Dr. Downing then goes on to refer to some of the reports of Major Donald Keyhoe, such as flying saucers seeming to disappear into a dark object that was apparently a "mother-ship":[8]

> But given the idea of the "curvature" of space, and of an "inside" and "outside" universe, it would be possible to speculate that the so-called mother-ship into which the saucers flew was in fact the bend or warp in the space-time continuum, some kind of space "tunnel" from the "middle" universe to either the "inside" or "outside" universe.

Some might suggest there is an overlap between this theory of a parallel world free of our gravitational restrictions, and the possibility of electromagnetic power which utilizes antigravitational propulsion—not from a world having the same space continuum, but rather from some other planet beyond this earth's "boundaries."

The theory of a parallel world is interesting, and Dr. Downing goes on to discuss a number of controversial topics. It is not our purpose to debate, nor to state our agreement or our disagreement. We are simply indicating that there are alternative points of view, and one is that there is a "parallel" universe to our own, occupying the same space continuum, though normally unknown to most of us.

Do They Come from Another Planet?

Many people who accept the fact of UFOs believe that they come from another planet, and at first sight the evidence seems substantial. Many of the personnel involved with United States Air Force and other defense investigations have given serious consideration to the possibility that the saucers come from outer space.

We have already seen that Donald Keyhoe put it to Captain (later Admiral) Fahrney that some air force officers had earlier suggested the possibility of the saucers coming from Russia. Fahrney had answered flatly that

that was impossible, and that the statement had been a hasty reaction, given before the implications had been thought out—that no matter how many former Nazi scientists had been kidnapped, the Soviet could not possibly have progressed to be so far ahead of the United States. Keyhoe reports Fahrney as saying, "No, either the saucers don't exist—and those reports are hard to brush off—or else they're interplanetary."[9]

Keyhoe himself became convinced that this was the only explanation, and came out publicly with that conclusion. He hesitated before committing himself fully, then came out with an article in a national magazine. He knew that if that article drew only ridicule his personal reputation would be seriously tarnished. Nevertheless he felt that the evidence was such that he must make his conclusions public, and he went ahead. He tells of the hubbub that followed the article's publication, and of a special interview being arranged with a prominent writer and a United States Air Force Intelligence officer. Questions were asked specifically about some of the cases which Keyhoe had stated were unresolved.

The air force explanation in one case involving an air force pilot was that he was killed chasing the planet Venus; another supposedly unexplained case was no problem because the witnesses had merely seen a meteor as it raced past; and in a third case the pilot was chasing nothing more than a lighted weather balloon. When pinned down as to the fact that Venus was practically invisible in the hours of the day when the first incident took place, the air force intelligence officer insisted that there was no other possible answer—and so the pilot must have been killed chasing Venus. The other two cases had earlier been investigated by an air force project before they were listed as "unsolved" in an official release. The intelligence officer acknowledged that no new facts had been discovered, but said that a new analysis had been made, and these were the answers they now stood by.

That intelligence officer had been put on the spot at

a time when it was extremely difficult to decide what the official U.S. policy should be as to information released to the public. The experience of the Orson Welles broadcast years before was constantly in the minds of many officials, and there was very good reason to believe that public panic might follow statements such as an admission that UFOs might come from outer space. In those days at the end of the 1940s and the early 1950s, official spokesmen could hardly win. Keyhoe goes on to analyze the answers given in those three cases, and suggests that some other answer must be looked for.

In retrospect, it would appear that Keyhoe was right. At the same time it should be pointed out that many cases that air force personnel investigated did indeed turn out to have logical explanations such as hallucinations, hoaxes, sightings of weather balloons, temperature inversion effects on clouds, and even mass hysteria and delusion.

Keyhoe had unusual cooperation from air force personnel, but it was a considerable time before he got the acknowledgment he wanted. It is not until almost the end of his outstanding book that he shows that the U.S. Air Force did take seriously the interplanetary argument. He quotes[10] an official air force memorandum, admittedly cautious in its wording, but concluding on the note "that if the apparently controlled maneuvers reported by many competent observers are correct, then the only remaining explanation is the interplanetary answer." In many of the reports officially handed out, the fact of such controlled maneuvers was accepted, and, as Keyhoe states, this was an official air force admission that the saucers came from space: hundreds of veteran pilots had sworn to such maneuvers, and simultaneous radar and visual tracking had proved it beyond question.

Remember, these points were made in the first edition of this book—before the Freedom of Information Act. What then sounded like fantasy is now established as fact.

Watchers from Space!

In the record of the discussion that follows, the intelligence officer who issued the report (Mr. Albert M. Chop) stated that he personally had been convinced for a long time that the saucers were interplanetary—that there was no other possible answer. Mr. Chop stated:[11]

One thing's absolutely certain—we're being watched by beings from outer space. You've been right from the very start.

At that time Mr. Chop was resigning his intelligence position, and for some years he was actively associated with Donald Keyhoe in an organization heading up space research. It is relevant to note that the time came when Mr. Chop resigned from that organization, apparently because he could no longer accept his earlier-held belief that the vehicles were interplanetary.

It is now many years since Donald Keyhoe's conclusions were reached, for in his epilogue he states that the fateful year of 1954 was approaching. Although twenty years have passed, earth has not been invaded. In that epilogue, Keyhoe suggests that investigation of UFOs should be expanded, and he urges that top-level scientists should be involved.

That actually happened, and eventually the Condon Report was published in January, 1969. When the results of the investigation were made known, the theory of electromagnetism and of visitors from other universes lost many of its adherents. We shall see that the scientific investigation led to quite opposite conclusions. As a result of that investigation, there were a number who quietly studied the facts, and then withdrew. Scientists suddenly found that they had too many other projects to be involved in, and decided they could not lend their names to anything associated with "flying saucers." One major reason was that they accepted the basic conclusions of the Condon Report—and they knew their own reputations could be affected if they were identified with paraphysical phenomena.

Not all accepted the Condon Report, and among ufologists there has been much criticism of it. Many regarded it as simply a great exercise in government whitewashing. Numbers have ridiculed it, sometimes quite unfairly, as though it had simply come to the conclusion that there were no flying saucers and that the answer always was "hallucination." However, that is not what the Condon Report came to. It concluded that the objects were just as "material" as any other physical objects, though perhaps only temporarily so. It claimed that the phenomena of flying saucers was in the same category as mysteries associated with séances and spiritist movements. This we shall elaborate in another chapter on paraphysical phenomena.

If it was ever actually established that saucers did come from other planets, all sorts of consequences would follow. Governments would raise taxes to a level never before known, to rush programs for the construction of defense missiles, and to achieve technological skills on a scale never before undertaken. There would probably even be cooperation between the nations of earth, such as would not otherwise be expected. Some religious teachings would be reanalyzed, as to what effect this would have on traditional views which tended to limit life to this one planet, with "intelligent" life enjoyed only by man. Land values would undergo great changes, and possibly less populous areas would become outrageously dear as people sought to get away from cities and other places where the saucers might be expected to land or attack.

Different Space Bases

Another theory sometimes put forward by ufologists is that these vehicles in fact come from a number of different bases in space—some might be friendly to earth and others hostile. Some might be looking for new sources of supply of rare minerals such as uranium, others might be mapping our defense bases with a view to later attack; others again might simply be checking on our life, possibly to show an interest sociologically; or perhaps they are conducting biological experiments, including the gathering of live specimens from the human, animal, and plant kingdoms. Some might be warning of the potential dangers if atomic and hydrogen bombs continue to be exploded.

A number of ufologists suggest it is taking considerable time for these saucer people to analyze us and to come to conclusions about us, because we are so different from themselves. Whatever the reason, there are many who fear that no preparations whatever have been made for when these people show themselves in strength. There is a common fear that we would have no realistic defense whatever.

There have been many attempts to make radio contact with these supposed beings from outer space. One humorous incident is reported in *Spacelink*:[12]

A few days after the 1967 National Sky Watch Day documentary was screened on BBC TV "Panorama," Mr. Colin McCarthy had two strange visitors. They were from the GPO's Wireless Licensing Department, and expressed great concern at Mr. McCarthy's attempts to establish radio communication with UFOs. They pointed out that this attempt was contravening their regulations, as UFOs were not licensed by the GPO.

Perhaps the UFOs could not respond to radio signals because the occupants' hands were tied by some sort of interplanetary red tape!

Others suggest that in fact contact is often made. We have said that sometimes space writers refer to three men in black—supposedly visitors from another planet who usually dress in black, able to assume the forms of men, and to pass virtually unnoticed in the large cities of the world. One of those who claims to have had experiences with these men is Albert K. Bender. Bender is one of the main subjects of Gray Barker's book *They Knew Too Much About Flying Saucers*—Barker did his best to find out all about UFOs from Bender, but for some time was quite unsuccessful.

Then some years later Bender tells his story, introduced by Gray Barker, in *Flying Saucers and the Three Men*. Bender claims he was not free to reveal his story at the time of the earlier book, for he had been threatened with dire consequences if he revealed the secret of the UFO visitants. He had been given a metal disk, and could contact the space personnel at any time by pressing that disk. Eventually the spacemen left this planet, and Bender knew he was free to tell his story, for he found that the disk had disappeared, as he had been told it would.

He then claimed that the visitors were from another planet, and that they were visiting earth to take a secret compound that was found in the vast areas of the oceans of the earth. Bender's story reads like a fantastic novel, and many would reject it out of hand. He tells of instant teleportation into a secret cavern where he met a being who was virtually worshipped by the others of the group, and this being supposedly answered many of Bender's questions.

Bender himself underwent all sorts of ridicule and rejection as the result of his story, but it is entirely possible that, if there was deception, it was Bender himself who was deceived. He retained his secret for about ten years before revealing it, supposedly after the disk had disappeared, and in some ways it is a frightening story.

In his introduction to Bender's book, Gray Barker states that he submitted the manuscript to a close friend of UFO research who could not be named because of his public position. According to Barker:[18]

His first reaction upon reading parts of the edited and unedited manuscript pages was that the book sounded much like science fiction. As he read further and more carefully, however, he became convinced that Bender was telling the truth. I was most interested in this first reaction to Bender's book, and I believe that in general it will be the most common.

Housing UFOs in the USA!

This actually is the impression an unbiased reader
tends to get as he reads through the book—not necessarily to believe that it all happened, but at least to believe that Bender believes that it happens. At that point
the reader himself becomes the interpreter—if he accepts the concept that these vehicles are from outer
space, powered by the utilization of electromagnetic
fields, then he might very well accept Bender's story as
totally factual. If he accepts the paraphysical argument,
he might decide that Bender's experience was entirely
real, but that it was basically an experience in his own
mind rather than of physical transportation to a
strange, huge cavern where a great fleet of UFOs was
housed, apparently somewhere in the United States.

It is of course hard to believe that so many fantastic
vehicles could be housed under the very eyes of the
greatest power on earth, without even the site itself
being known. It is also hard to accept that such fantastic interplanetary machines would so often be breaking down, and even dropping parts off from time to
time. Why do they not fly back to that secret base in
the United States that Bender described so clearly?

It is also peculiar that these sightings are so often reported in fairly prominent places such as highways, and
that usually the vehicles take off as soon as they have
been observed. It almost seems that they are anxious to
promote the belief that they are engaged in repair activities—otherwise, why do they not land in less populous
areas? Many of the contactees claim there is some television-type scanning system on board. Why then land
so often in such "obvious" places? We have already
suggested that possibly this is part of their tactics.

There are many of these "repair" stories from the
1897 flap to more modern sightings—including the famous New Guinea sighting by Reverend William Gill
and thirty-seven witnesses. Would fantastic interplanetary machines really keep breaking down, and yet

never be "captured"? It rather seems it is a way of impressing the fact of their actuality on earth-beings!

Another repair story was recounted by Reinhold Schmidt on November 5, 1957.[14] His car had stalled outside Kearney in Nebraska, and when he got out to check it he was surprised to see a silver "blimp" in a field nearby. He was spoken to by one of the occupants, in perfect German, which he understood, and was informed that repairs were being made. He was told only vaguely about who the occupants were, but was assured that he would know eventually—this is the same sort of report that was made by various contactees at the time of the 1897 "flap."

Although Schmidt's story was regarded as the product of a disturbed mind, puddles of a purple liquid and visible indentations were found where he claimed the object had stood. Both these aspects have been common with many supposed sightings, and although Schmidt himself has to some extent been criticized as a result of later events, it seems highly possible that his basic story was true.

Which Planet?

The question is often asked, "If UFOs come from outer space, where do they come from?" A number of ufologists have claimed that there is a planet Clarion on the "other" side of the moon, between the earth and the sun. This is simply not possible to accept because of the constantly changing relationship of these three bodies. In any case, manned flights around the moon have disproved the theory.

Others suggest the planet Mars, but the 1969 Mariner probe indicated that temperature, etc., on Mars was not conducive to life as we know it, so that suggestion has been put to one side. Captain David C. Holmes, USN, is quoted by space writers as having played a key part in the space program of the U.S. government, and he writes concerning two stars about eleven light-years away from earth—Tau Ceti and Epsilon Eridani.[15] Some ufologists suggest that these are the bases from which UFOs have supposedly been visiting earth for the last twenty years and more. Some with less scientific knowledge have referred to Venus, the Pleiades, and various other possible homes from outer space. The accumulating evidence tends to discount such possibilities.

When Mariner II passed about 22,000 miles from Venus in December, 1962, its instruments measured the surface temperature of that planet as about 800°F—thus Venus is certainly too hot to sustain life as we know it.

Most ufologists agree that Jupiter would hardly be the place where space visitors came from—despite some of the fantastic stories. The temperature of Jupiter is extremely cold, and in any case the gravity pull on Jupiter is about two and a half times stronger than that on the earth. Anyone landing from Jupiter on the earth would have to be heavily weighted down, and the reports of "space beings" certainly do not indicate that this has been the case. Similar arguments can be advanced against the visitors coming from Uranus, Neptune, and Saturn. Pluto is always in darkness and is extremely cold, whereas Mercury is too close to the sun—on one side of it humanoid creatures would be roasted, while on the other they would be frozen.

The fact that these adverse reports about atmospheric and climatic conditions on Mars and other planets have been made has not dulled the enthusiasm of some ufologists. They suggest that superintelligent beings would have ways of scientifically controlling or adjusting themselves to whatever physical conditions there might be on a particular planet. They also argue that these beings might merely be using (e.g.) Mars as a base—they do not insist that the beings themselves are necessarily original inhabitants of Mars.

Other confirmed ufologists, especially those who believe some of the fantastic stories about earthlings visiting some of these planets, suggest that the body cells of those planetarians might be constituted differently from those of earthlings—e.g., having silicon instead of carbon as the essential constituent of their cells, as is the case with earth-bound life. They argue that this would make it possible to endure temperatures greatly different from those on the earth.

It is also relevant that ufologists are suggesting bases that are at least several light-years away. The point is often made that beings from those planets could never reach us in a lifetime because of the impossibility of going beyond the speed of light. At this point we repeat that in this volume we are attempting to put forward facts and to suggest possible answers. At times those possible answers seem so way-out that one wonders if they should even be mentioned. However, scientific knowledge has advanced fantastically in this generation, and technology is such that we no longer say that concepts at present beyond our understanding or knowledge are therefore impossible to achieve. Perhaps this is relevant as to the possibility of future (or even present!) interplanetary travel.

The Advances of Technology

The renowned Einstein stated that at about 186,000 miles per second—that being the speed of light—mass would become infinite, and one result would be that time would come to a stop. It is entirely possible that scientists will come to accept the possibility of speed beyond the speed of light, and one surprising concept is teleportation. This refers to instantaneous movement of a body from one place to another, even thousands or more miles away. There are reputable scientists who take this concept seriously, and in our chapter on paraphysical phenomena we shall refer to the possibility of this occurring in recent times. Ufologists claim that the U.S. government is researching the concept of teleportation quite seriously, calling it ITF, standing for Instant Transference.

Einstein's theory of special relativity is sometimes referred to as part of the explanation as to how extensive space travel could be undertaken. Even if man moved at the speed of light it would still take years to reach the nearest planetary system outside that which revolves around our own sun. However, there is possibly a loophole in what is known as the "time dilatation factor." The argument is that time shrinks as the speed of light is approached, so that the actual time lapsed (as earth-bound people think of time) would be considerably less than the time actually taken. However, there would still be fantastic periods of time involved.

Other ufologists bypass the problems, and simply suggest that we have made such advances technologically since the beginning of World War II that the thought of travel to other planetary systems must no longer be regarded as a fantastic impossibility.

All that is not to suggest that these visitors are in fact from another planet, and actually there is much evidence to the contrary. Over and over again the witnesses tell us that these strange beings blithely enter our atmosphere, breathe our air, speak our languages, and even wear clothes that fit in with the particular cultural patterns where they have landed. There is much more of this nature, and it is logical to ask how they adapt so readily. It is also difficult to know how, if there have been these sightings through so many centuries, there has not been a single case of a captured spacecraft, or of definitely established contacts at top levels, or of response to radio and other signals. The electromagnetism theory, combined with the argument that these beings come from other planets, is not entirely convincing.

Another explanation should be looked for. Many will disagree, and argue that the basic problems have been resolved by beings who utilize the principles of electromagnetism and are able to neutralize the force of gravity.

To that subject we now turn.

Chapter 11

Electromagnetic Power?
An Antigravitational Force?

Belief in UFOs leads to the obvious problem of their propulsion. Many researchers have concluded that the amazingly swift acceleration of these vehicles cannot be duplicated by anything made on earth. The speeds reliably estimated have been fantastic—as when two officials in a control tower at Terre Haute estimated the speed of one at 42,000 miles per hour. There was an independent confirmation of this sighting from an aircraft, when what was apparently the same vehicle was seen over an atomic energy plant at Newport in Indiana.

If we accept the incredible speeds so often reported, we must recognize that some previously unknown propulsion force is being utilized.

A New Propulsion Force?

In *The True Report on Flying Saucers,* Donald Keyhoe suggests that the startlingly swift acceleration of UFOs is a maneuver with only one possible explanation:[1]

According to many scientists and engineers, there is only one possible answer. The answer is *antigravity*: artificial gravity fields and control of gravity power.

He goes on to say that there have been forty-six U.S. government research projects set up to investigate the possibility of control of gravity. He points out that the value to whatever country first obtains it would be incalculable. He further makes the point that two significant facts have been established:[2]

1. The earth's G field is relatively weak, compared with the pull of gravity between planets and the sun.
2. There is a connection between gravity and electromagnetic fields.

One reputable authority who believed that electromagnetic power was linked with the answer was Wilbert B. Smith, who headed up the original Canadian "Saucer" Project. He is mentioned from time to time by space writers, including Donald Keyhoe who quotes Smith as believing that there were only three possibilities—that these craft were interplanetary, or were United States secret devices, or were a new Russian invention. He ruled out the second and third possibilities, and therefore believed the saucers could only come from outer space. In that same conversation he outlined to Keyhoe his own ideas as to the space vehicles' secret of propulsion as follows:[3]

First, let's consider the parent ship. From the high altitude sightings, I think it must be a type like this. For power it could use nuclear fission, mass conversion of energy, or some other revolutionary source, such as cosmic rays. But our experiments indicate that the two disks, which are probably launched from large parent ships, utilized magnetic fields of force. And it's possible that the parent ship also uses this same sort of power.

The possibility of electromagnetic propulsion had been considered seriously for some years previously, and over those years there had been strange reports such as compass needles going wild, and of spacecraft hovering over areas where they could apparently tap sources of power.

One theory was that the electricity of the ionosphere could be utilized. Experts say that in the upper atmosphere ions are actually stripped of some of the outer electrons by the action of the ultraviolet rays of the sun. The theory is that this ionization frees molecules which carry large electric charges, and that if this electric force could be tapped there would possibly be a form of propulsion that would be even better than atomic energy. When Wilbert Smith was asked for his reaction to the fact that some of these schemes for possible space travel had been ridiculed, he pointed out that this had been true with plans for the airplane, the helicopter, jets, the atom bomb, and many other modern developments. He himself was one of the leaders in a project to build a disk utilizing electromagnetism for its propulsion.

Keyhoe asked Smith for permission to use technical data associated with that project, and Smith agreed to do this as long as it was cleared by the Canadian government. Eventually Keyhoe was able to include an elaborate memorandum in his highly interesting *Flying Saucers from Outer Space*, partly quoted below. In his survey, Wilbert Smith said that this new technology in magnetics could offer an acceptable explanation for some of the striking features that had been reported with flying saucers. Smith wrote that it would be possible to produce a magnetic "sink" within the earth's own field—this would be a region into which the magnetic flux would flow at a controlled rate, and would give up some of its potential energy in the process. Some of the properties of such a sink would be as follow:[4]

1. Electrical power could be obtained from the collapse of the earth's magnetic field into the "sink."
2. Powerful reaction forces could be developed in a conducting ring surrounding the sink and offset from it, sufficient to support a suitably designed ship and to propel it.
3. If the rate of flow of magnetic flux is modulated, the resulting magnetic disturbances could be used for communication purposes.

Remote Control?

Smith pointed out that many descriptions of flying saucers fitted in with the design that would be necessary if the properties of a magnetic sink were exploited. He even associated the various colors such as red and white as fitting in with this theory of propulsion. He suggested that many of the close turns and maneuvers which were reported so often with flying saucers, resulting in large accelerations, would seem to indicate that the saucers were remotely controlled and therefore did not contain living matter as people of earth would know it.

Smith had an interesting theory about the color condition. He suggested:[5]

> Also, under certain conditions of operation a very high voltage may be built up between the center and the rim of the disk, which could result in a corona discharge through the surrounding air, if the saucer were at a sufficiently high altitude. Such a discharge would resemble the Northern Lights but would be very much more intense.

On Color Changes

Donald Keyhoe elaborates this color concept, and suggests that different colors would predominate, according to the height of the vehicle. At lower altitudes the corona discharge would be only short in length, and the color seen would be blue-white. At high altitudes it would tend to be green or bluish green, whereas when even higher in altitude it would possibly be red, yellow, blue, and green.

He puts forward elaborate evidence showing there is reason to believe there has been consistency as to color, size, and speed associated with flying saucers.[6]

Wilbert Smith had argued that if the rotation of the disk was swiftly accelerated, the human eye would not be able to catch the rapid changes from red to white, and the same would be true in reducing the rotation. If the slowing was gradual, various stages would be visible as the disk turned through yellow, orange, red, pink, and then finally became dark. If that rotation was abruptly slowed or even stopped, the cooling effect of the air at high speed would be so swift that the impression would be given of a light being turned off.

Such an explanation not only covered the night sightings, but was applicable to the daylight reports as well, for in the daylight most reports were that the objects were of some silver-colored metal. Thus in the daylight they would gleam in a similar way to conventional airplanes, although there would still be color changes that would not be detected so easily in the sunlight.

A typical example of color associated with UFOs was in an encounter near West Palm Beach on August 19, 1952.[7] Scout Master D. S. Desvergers with three scouts was driving home from a meeting when they saw a series of strange lights in nearby woods. Desvergers set out alone to investigate, and within about two minutes one of the scouts saw a ball of fire, reddish white in color, coming from about the top of a tree and slanting down toward where they had last seen Desvergers. The scout master did not return for some time, and one of the boys telephoned the sheriff.

The sheriff took the call seriously and answered it just in time to meet Desvergers as he staggered out of the woods, badly frightened and exhausted. He claimed that when he pointed his flashlight toward the disk over his head, a fiery spray had shot out from it, scorching his arms and burning his hat. He lay on the ground dazed for several minutes, and when he got up, the saucer had gone. His arm was reddened as though by heat, and his hat was in fact burned. There was a small scorched area where Desvergers claimed the disk had been.

This sort of burning has been associated with a number of other sightings—such as with two boys who reported seeing a small disk land at Amarillo in Texas. They claimed that its top section was still spinning. When one boy touched it, the rotating part speeded up and threw off some sort of hot gas or spray. The disk then took off at the usual very fast speed. This seemed to many to be an incredible story, but the boy had red burn spots on both his face and arms.

At the time, a number of people claimed that this sort of story could have been made up to cover some childish prank, and of course one of the problems in investigating UFO stories is that specific cases could be hoaxes. However, again we point out that there are so many similarities in details, similarities that could not be known to those who reported them, that it is logical to take some stories seriously.

Color Clues to Propulsion

Bringing the evidence together, it seems that the change of color of the "space vehicles" is possibly a clue to the way these space vehicles are propelled: they slow before they make a turn, and then brighten considerably as they accelerate.

A typical case was on July 29, 1952, when a yellow lighted saucer was sighted over the atomic energy base at Los Alamos.[8] When it was first sighted, it appeared to be hovering, but after about a minute it streaked away and its color changed from yellow to white. The vehicle disappeared in about fifteen seconds.

Another example of change of light was that reported by an air force pilot on November 26, 1952, when he chased a disk some miles from a base over Labrador.[9] The saucer turned to climb away and its color changed from bright red to white, and the same pilot witnessed a similar change some twenty days later when he tracked a second disk on his radar. This time the color changes were also witnessed by a second pilot.

Yet another example of color change was associated

with a sighting on July 14, 1953.[10] Pilots had actually flown above flying saucers, and with the earth beneath them as a background they had been able to make an accurate assessment of both the size and speed of the strange craft. The sky was clear, and there was unlimited visibility, with the distant lights of Norfolk, Virginia, visibly clear.

At first a strange reddish glow was noticed in the sky ahead, and only a moment later six disks were seen, glowing orange-red and approaching at the fantastic speed which is so commonly reported of UFOs. They seemed to be about 100 feet in diameter, and were flying in formation. One disk stopped abruptly, and there was a distinct dimming of its glow. A moment later they all changed direction as they streaked off into the night, and as they increased their speed, there was a pronounced brightening of their glow. Two of the disks had stopped behind, and when they accelerated to catch the others they glowed the brightest of all. Suddenly they all went dark, only to reappear as eight machines in one line. Then they headed out to the west, before climbing into the night sky and quickly disappearing.

Witnesses reported they had been some time over the city, as well as possibly observing the nearby naval base and naval air station. The way the reports were made, it was difficult to believe that the disks were not controlled and maneuvered by intelligent beings, whether on board the disks themselves or by remote control. It seemed clear that they could not have been manned by earthlings, it being argued that no human beings could have stood the violent shocks that must have accompanied the maneuverings of the flying objects.

However, as scientific knowledge has increased, experiments and then actual space exploration have shown that humans can stand far more "Gs" than had once been believed—we pointed out earlier that one "G" is the pull normally exerted by gravity on beings on the earth. As early as 1950, ideas were being put forward along the lines of rotating spaceships, whereby "inside" compartments would be protected from non-normal gravitation pull. Nevertheless, many top scientists have insisted that humanoids could not withstand the pressures involved with the electromagnetic propulsion that is apparently utilized by these craft.

According to present knowledge, electromagnetism could give only part of the answer for UFO maneuvering. If it is put forward as the explanation to all the problems, there are questions relating to a number of matters, such as that of an invisible repelling force, to which many witnesses have referred. This has prevented them approaching too close to the vehicle or to the strange beings they had come across—one such example being Nathan Brown of Awanui, in the far north of New Zealand. It is hard to know where fact and fiction merge in some of the reported incidents: their strangeness does not necessarily make them incredible.

Fact or Fiction?

One report that caught the public eye was made by a Pueblo radio executive named Joseph Rohrer.[11] He claimed that seven flying disks had come into the hands of the government, three of them having been forced down in the state of Montana. He reported that the saucers were giant rotating disks, together with stationary cabins, and that he himself had been inside one. He described it as being over 100 feet in diameter and 18 feet thick, put together in five sections, with the crew's sleeping quarters consisting of tubes that had caps on the ends.

Rohrer stated that the cabins were pressured with 30 percent oxygen mixed with 70 percent helium, and that the vehicles depended on electrostatic turbines for their propulsion, while the magnetic fields created by the rotating rings of the vehicles themselves made their tremendous speed possible. According to Rohrer, the different colors that were so frequently seen in the space vehicles were caused by the variations of speed. He claimed that the UFOs avoided close approaches over cities, and even to airplanes, in order to minimize interference with electrical appliances. U.S. Air Force representatives claimed they knew nothing of the disks which Rohrer described.

Fact or fiction? Much of what he described is along the lines which the proponents of electromagnetism suggest. Has someone done some research and then put it to good use with this interesting "sighting"? Or was Joseph Rohrer deceived by some nonhuman force? Did he dream his "experience"—or was it real, at least to him? With many such incidents the questions can be asked, but the answers are not always clear.

In recent years John Keel has carefully analyzed the color aspect, and the change of appearance in nighttime as against daytime is interestingly illustrated by one case he discusses. He tells of two Pennsylvania policemen named William Ruttledge and Donald Peck who watched a strange light for two hours on August 3, 1966.[12] They first saw it at 4.45 A.M. as a bright light that was moving eastward and then stopped, turned red, and finally disappeared. It reappeared a moment later and was a bluish white color. They watched it until 6.55 A.M. and then, as the sun came up and the sky was flooded with light, the strange phenomenon ceased being only a light—it now could be seen as a silvery object, possibly metallic in structure. They saw it heading off over Lake Erie toward Canada, and then it disappeared.

Keel presents two very interesting charts relating the electromagnetic spectrum to a series of rays—cosmic rays, gamma rays, X-rays, ultraviolet rays, visible light rays, heat waves, and radio waves; the second chart relates to visible light and the color spectrum—ultraviolet light is invisible and can burn skin and eyes, and then there is a progress through violet to blue, cyan (bluish green), green, yellow, red, magenta (purplish red) and infrared (invisible), heat waves, and radio waves.[13]

He relates both these charts to the appearance and disappearance of UFOs, and discusses similarities between light waves and radio waves. Light waves are actually visible vibrations of the spectrum, with different frequencies registering as different colors on the cones of the human eye. There is a great deal around us we do not see, but what we do see is sufficient to cope with our immediate environment. Even ultraviolet rays are invisible apart from special glasses, but can burn flesh and eyes alike. Many of those who claim to have witnessed UFOs have reported that they have suffered symptoms of burning, with red eyes, itching sensations, and other signs of burning on their skin. The incidents are very plentiful, and the evidence becomes conclusive that ultraviolet waves are associated with these objects in a way that would not be true of a man-made object, stars, satellites, etc.

Keel makes the point that visible light comes between ultraviolet and heat waves, and he tells how many contactees and witnesses of UFOs have complained of oppressive waves of heat associated with the vehicle overhead or on the ground. In normal circumstances, humans are protected from the dangerous effects of the electromagnetic spectrum by the Van Allen radiation belt that circles the earth, and by the atmosphere itself, which strains out cosmic rays as they constantly bombard earth dwellers. He links the entry field of UFOs with violet blue and cyan (bluish green), leading on to green, yellow, and red. The UFO departure field is tied in with magenta (purplish red) before the invisible infrared ray stage is reached.

Basic Principles of Electromagnetism

Keel has an excellent summary of the basic principles associated with UFOs and electromagnetics:[14]

1. All solid matter in our environment (or reality) is composed of energy.
2. All energies are of an electromagnetic nature.

3. The human eye can perceive only a very small portion of the electromagnetic spectrum.
4. Electromagnetic waves of many different frequencies permeate the known universe.

We live in a sea of such radiations, and the space through which our planet travels is an ocean of radiation.

He goes on to discuss the fact that telescopes have discovered that space is filled with infrared rays whose origin is unknown, and even "invisible" stars have been detected with infrared devices. The reason for their being invisible is simply that they do not issue rays that we can see within our limited frequencies of the visible light spectrum. Their energies are radiated in higher frequencies (such as X-rays) and lower frequencies (such as radio waves).

Keel has a comment at the end of this section which to many would be frightening in its implications. He states:[15]

Somewhere in this tangled mass of electromagnetic frequencies there lies an omnipotent intelligence, however. This intelligence is able to manipulate energy. It can, quite literally, manipulate any kind of object into existence on our plane. For centuries the occultists and religionists have called this process transmutation or transmogrification.

He links some of these transmogrifications of energy to such concepts as poltergeist manifestations—noisy ghosts—and the mysterious fires that sometimes take place in "haunted" houses. According to Keel, many fires whose origin is undetermined have erupted suddenly in UFO flap areas.

On the surface, it would seem that the electromagnetism theory would explain why motor cars and other vehicles have been stalled when UFOs have been nearby.[16] However, it appears that this is not the answer. Keel investigated the subject in depth, and makes this report:[17]

A tremendous amount of magnetism would be required to produce the magnetic effects blamed on the objects, such as the stalling of automobiles. The Ford Motor Company, working with a UFO investigating group at Colorado University, discovered that simple magnetism could not stall an auto engine encased in the protective steel body of a car. A field strong enough to accomplish this would also be strong enough to bend the car itself and possibly affect the passengers as well.

Perhaps it should be stressed, however, that the Ford investigation does not rule out the influence of UFOs on vehicles, but rather deals with one of the theories *about* UFOs. The investigation has special relevance to the effect of electromagnetic power. If the Ford conclusions are unanswerable, this simply means that the electromagnetic theory does not offer a complete solution as to how UFOs are powered: for there are many cases where motor car engines were undoubtedly stalled as a result of a UFO being present. The Ford inquiry actually adds strength to the paraphysical explanation.

If electromagnetism is the total answer, this would seem to demand belief that these beings come from other planets. However, over and over again the reports of contacts with humanoids show that they breathe the air on earth, usually without any helmet-type covering, and adapt to our gravity with no trouble at all. Some reports tell of humanoids gliding across a field (or even inside their spaceships), but in the main they are supposed to walk and move and breathe just as though they had been on earth for all time.

Engine Stallings Should Be Studied

Dr. Hynek is another highly reputable researcher who calls for investigation and analysis of such associated matters as color changes and engine stalling. Apart from an epilogue, his significant book concludes with suggestions as to patterns of investigation that should be followed. He says that in the hundreds of cases where there has been reported failure of automobiles in

146

the presence of UFOs, investigators should check what factors they had in common—and in what ways they differed. They should ask such questions as, "Which failed first, the radio, the lights, or the motor?"

He also suggests that there should be serious study of the frequency of colors manifested with the UFOs, and this fits into the pattern suggested by John Keel in his fascinating book, *UFOs ... Operation Trojan Horse*. Dr. Hynek also links the color frequencies with the speeds of various UFOs. He then states:[18]

> Such analyses, coupled with the *active* program of on-the-spot investigations of a truly scientific character, should accomplish the first objective of a positive UFO program: to establish the reality of the UFO as a legitimate subject for further scientific study. If definite patterns and other correlations can be established for UFOs reported in many different countries by people with different levels of culture, the probability that such correlations happen by chance as a result of random misperceptions would be vanishingly small. The probability, therefore, that the UFO represents something truly new in science—new empirical observations—would be a virtual certainty.

We repeat, this statement comes from a first-class scientist who laughed with so many others at the very thought of flying saucers, who became an official UFO consultant to the U.S. Air Force, but now boldly declares that flying saucers should be taken seriously.

Some who believe that UFOs are powered by electromagnetic force point to potential dangers at various levels. If a flying disk utilizing electromagnetism were to fly low over a city, it could cause all sorts of damage to power lines and metal surfaces, with fuses blown and wires burnt out. Even motor car engines and airplanes could be affected if the space vehicle came close enough. Those who argue that the saucers are friendly have pointed out in this connection that inhabited areas have been largely avoided by low-flying disks, but that argument is not entirely valid. There have been very many sightings over large cities.

the presence of UFOs, investigators should expect what factors they had in common—and in what ways they differed. They should ask such questions as, "Which would be the effects on the lights...

A Paradox

One paradox in all this is that only some of these consequences have followed. Again we point out that the electromagnetic explanation is not convincing at all points, though clearly the principle is being utilized to some extent.

Donald Keyhoe outlined conversations with Canadian expert Wilbert Smith in which he discussed various other UFO topics, such as the possibilities of television scanners and cameras, and of locking small disks into the mother craft so that they could be held magnetically by various forms of robot control. He suggested that the split-second delays, reported by many pilots before spacecraft made their dramatic turns, occurred while the robot analyst checked what forces should be utilized.[19]

Experts recognize very serious problems associated with this form of propulsion. If a hostile earth power were to discover the secret, all other powers would be at a serious disadvantage. The door would be open to dreadful guided missiles which no power could withstand.

Even present space projects could be utilized in ways that are dreadful to consider. One of the possibilities with electromagnetic power would be that the moon could become a base on which guided missiles were stored and then easily launched, the moon's gravity being only one sixth that of the earth. The missiles could be guided by radar to any target on earth.

The moon could also be a base for moving off to other space destinations. UFOs could be engaged in reconnaissance flights over the earth, the moon being the base from which that reconnaissance was undertaken. The reconnaissance could include the mapping of strategic areas such as power and defense centers, etc. Much of this is possible in embryo with present, more conventional forms of propulsion and technical know-how, but the argument is that the potential, if

148

ever the propulsion secret of UFOs becomes known, is frightening.

However, all this presumes that UFOs are powered by electromagnetic propulsion. Not all scientists who "believe" in UFOs accept that that *is* the answer, and there is an alternative. In some ways it is even more frightening if we are prepared to face it, but many, even highly intelligent people, are not.

To that alternative we now turn.

Chapter 12

The Paraphysical Explanation

NOTE—Some of the concepts dealt with in this and the next chapter are so "way-out" that a number of other writers are quoted extensively. This is to make it clear that these are not the unsupported views of this writer. At the same time it should be stressed that the interpretations are his own.

One reason why many scientists and others continue to accept the electromagnetism interplanetary argument is that, for them, there is no acceptable alternative. Strangely, even that would have been considered unacceptable just a few years ago, for who would have seriously considered that we could be visited by humanoids from outer space?

Yet even that explanation would be considered "respectable" when put alongside the other most likely alternative—an alternative given some degree of scientific respectability by the Condon Report, published in January, 1969. That report resulted from a project, sponsored by the U.S. Air Force, for the scientific investigation of UFOs. It was headed by Dr. E. U. Condon of the University of Colorado. One of its main conclusions was that many sightings of UFOs, and contacts with UFO occupants, should be attributed to paraphysical phenomena. Let it be stated clearly that the Condon Report has been strenuously challenged—e.g., Chapter 12 of Dr. Hynek's book[1] is one such attack.

Our purpose is neither to defend nor to attack the report as such, but rather to suggest reasons why the paraphysical explanation should be considered just as seriously as the electromagnetism argument. We recognize the criticism that some members of the Condon Committee appear to have prejudged issues, and that not enough representative cases were studied. However, even if all the criticisms heaped against this group from the University of Colorado are true, that would not necessarily debunk the rightness of their basic conclusions.

Problems on Two Sides

In reading through some of the attacks against the report, one gets the impression that the "other" side have also—at least to some extent—prejudged the issue, in that they have decided that UFOs *are* a physical phenomenon of the most permanent variety, in the fullest earth-bound sense of the term. Perhaps some of them, too, are wrong, at least to the extent to which they too rule out the possibility of the paraphysical answer. Such a possibility has been somewhat reluctantly recognized in "official" U.S. circles for over twenty years.

Even as far back as 1952, when there was a serious effort to debunk the whole concept of flying saucers, General Samford of U.S. Intelligence referred obliquely to the parallel with spiritism, where competent and credible observers reported incredible things. He did not suggest that UFOs were in the same category, but suggested that the two had overtones of similarity, in that they were beyond usual explanations.[2]

Very early in the study of flying saucers in modern times, intelligence personnel have recognized that it simply would not be possible for any power—whether on earth or from another planet—to maintain the fantastic number of vehicles that were apparently involved, operating as they were right around the world. Although official statements have attempted to debunk the whole matter, it has been obvious for many years that the things were very "real." We have seen that witnesses included pilots and top military men, and even entire ships' crews had clearly observed something that was being maneuvered and directed by intelligent beings. However, they also knew that these things did not obey normal physical laws. For example, even though they were double-checked at speeds exceeding the speed of sound, there were no reports of sonic booms being heard—though this has been challenged in ufology circles.[3]

The maneuvers that these UFOs performed often defied the laws of inertia, and they would appear and disappear instantaneously, as though they were some spirit form. In the main, intelligence personnel were able to explain away most of the sightings to the satisfaction of members of the public, but very often that "satisfaction" excluded those who were the actual witnesses of the specific sightings!

Dr. Meade Layne had suggested the possibility that flying saucers involved paraphysical concepts in the early 1950s. The English science writer, Arthur C. Clarke, also wrote articles suggesting that the answers were in the realm of paraphysics rather than of extraterrestrial visitations. There were others, but in the main their hypotheses and arguments were rejected by ufologists. However, the evidence was of such a nature that it demanded serious investigation, and by 1955 many highly qualified investigators had considered the evidence and, as we have already seen, they had quietly withdrawn from further participation. It seems that many believed the mystery had been resolved, and they themselves were not anxious to be associated with answers that linked flying saucers with such phenomena as ghosts, spiritism, séances, and so much else they regarded as outside their expertise. For many of those serious investigators, to be associated with such beliefs would mean running the risk of being branded as emotionally disturbed, weird cultists, etc.

The 1980s have seen changes. Although not "respectable" in many circles, the paranormal must at least be taken seriously. But there is still resistance.

Opposing Opinions

It should be stated, as implied above, that there are many scientists who are not totally convinced by the Condon Report, partly because of claims that the committee's methods of investigation did not stand up to the searching tests of scientific objectivity. It is widely believed that there was considerable friction within the group itself, that conclusions were prejudged before their time, and that there were insufficient case studies involving statistical analysis and coordination. The American Institute of Aeronautics and Astronautics is one prestigious body which suggested that the UFO controversy is not yet resolved by the Condon Report, and that there are substantial numbers of unexplained observations which should not be ignored.

On the other hand, not all reviews were unfavorable. *Time* magazine of January 17, 1969, stated that the investigation had been thoroughly reviewed and then approved by the National Academy of Sciences—"Thus, when the *scientific study of unidentified flying objects* was finally made public last week, it spoke with authority." Its succinct comments summarized the position very well for those who accepted it:

> Its conclusions all but demolished the idea that earth has been visited by creatures from other planets. Despite a few remaining puzzles, there is no evidence, said the report, that UFOs are spaceships from extraterrestrial civilizations, and no scientific justification at this time for any further extensive saucer investigations.

As a result of the report, the phenomenon of UFOs has been downgraded in interest. Though many sightings are still reported, the Condon Report has had the side effect of brainwashing many people into believing that UFOs simply do not exist.

The fact that so many highly qualified scientific personnel lost interest and dropped out did not alter the reality of the phenomenon, its continuing occurrence, and the possible validity of the paraphysical answer. John Keel quotes RAF Air Marshal Lord Dowding, famous because it was he who directed the Battle of Britain in 1940, as publicly stating that the occupants of the UFOs were immortal: they could render themselves invisible to human eyes, though they could also take on human form and walk and work among human beings quite unnoticed.[4] This was an extraordinary statement to make, for Air Marshal Dowding had earlier circulated his strongly held view that the UFOs were extraterrestrial visitants.

Morris K. Jessup issued a number of books during the 1950s in which he discussed correlations of sightings, leading to the conclusion that the phenomena could be explained only in paraphysical terms. John Keel lists a number of other investigations which came to similar conclusions.[5] He claims that the only hypothesis that can answer all sightings is the paraphysical one, and that this is not true of the hypothesis that the UFOs are visitors from outer space.

Keel also suggests that UFO enthusiasts have rejected much of the real evidence, and in a sense have even suppressed it by ignoring relevant material which points to a different conclusion from what they expected. Keel suggests they have thereby made the problem more confusing, though not deliberately—that there was simply an unawareness of the very real evidence that pointed to the acceptability of the paraphysical hypothesis. That is shown by such theories as one that was put forward in all seriousness—to the effect that interested government departments were "arranging" for people to see flying saucers, deliberately utilizing this phenomenon as one of the subversionary tactics of the Cold War.

An Explosion of Knowledge

The fact is, there was an explosion of relevant data as to the paraphysical phenomenon in 1955, and from that time onward institutions such as the U.S. Air

Force have paid less attention to UFOs. Professional writers have tended to desert the subject, and since then UFO literature has included much that was pseudoscientific, and at times pure amateur speculation.

Some of the well-known names in UFO research were convinced that the paraphysical explanation should be considered seriously. Kenneth Arnold, the pilot who reported his sighting of UFOs in June, 1947, investigated UFOs for some years. Eight years after his famous sighting he issued a number of statements to the effect that the objects appeared to be some form of living energy that were not necessarily "spaceships" as we would think of them.[6]

Earlier we referred to Albert M. Chop, who issued a statement to Donald Keyhoe as to the apparent interplanetary nature of the UFO phenomenon. Eventually he withdrew his name from Major Keyhoe's organization, known as the National Investigation Committee on Aerial Phenomena, and publicly declared that he could no longer accept the theory that flying saucers were real physical machines. He was but one of the many who had come to the point where they realized they could not explain the phenomena in terms of known material objects.

Another who came to espouse the paraphysical answer was Royal Air Force Air Marshal Sir Victor Goddard, K.C.B., C.B.E., M.A., a member of the British cabinet who had been active in the Royal Air Force investigations into UFOs from 1950-1955. In a public lecture given at Caxton Hall in London, May 3, 1969, he stated that there was no logical need to believe that the operators of UFOs came from a planet other than earth:[7]

> For, if the materiality of UFO is paraphysical (and consequently normally invisible), UFO could more plausibly be creations of an invisible world coincident with the space of our physical earth planet that creations in the paraphysical realms of any other physical planet in the solar system. . . . Given that UFO are paraphysical, capable of reflecting lifelike ghosts; and

given also that (according to many observers) they remain visible as they change position at ultra high speeds from one point to another, it follows that those that remain visible in transition do not materialize for that swift back transition, and therefore, their mass must be of a diaphanous (very diffuse) nature, and their substance relatively etheric. . . . The observed validity of this supports the paraphysical assertion and makes the likelihood of UFO being earth-created greater than the likelihood of their creation on another planet.

Describing UFOs—Solid?

John Keel has coordinated much statistical data about UFOs, and reports his material so objectively that he should be listened to. He comments:[8]

The statistical data which I have extracted, which I have tried to summarize briefly here, indicate that flying saucers are *not* stable machines requiring fuel, maintenance, and logistical support. They are, in all probability, transmogrifications of energy and do not exist in the same way that this book exists. They are not permanent constructions of matter.

Transmogrifications of energy refer to the manipulation of molecules so that the energy is made visible in a new form. Transmogrifications refer to material apparitions. They can literally be composed of energies from the higher reaches of the mysterious electromagnetic spectrum. With the UFO phenomenon, this implies a superintelligence so that energies can be manipulated and reduced to visible frequencies, and take forms that have physical actualities as far as earth-bound beings are concerned.

Many of the reports of witnesses indicate that at least some UFOs were transparent, yet at the same time appearing to have mechanical or physical properties. There are strange stories of saucer occupants walking through the sides of their vehicles as though they themselves were ghosts. Much of the evidence suggests the possibility that the vehicles themselves, and even the occupants of those vehicles, are not "permanent" solids in the sense that we would think of vehicles and beings of the earth.

This is not to suggest that many of those vehicles are not solid at the time they are witnessed—we are not arguing that all sightings of UFOs are hallucinations or illusions, for at the time they are sighted many of them are just as "solid" as houses and motor cars and other objects of earth all around us. They can leave impressions of their tripod stands in the earth, and they can be touched and handled, and many contacts claim to have done just that. However, it seems that they can also be changed so that their molecular structure materializes or dematerializes in a way that we limited humans could not do. We do somewhat similar things on a lesser scale by utilizing such processes as fire so that objects can be melted or hardened into a different form. Similarly, a "solid" object can be transformed into a liquid, or even into a gas, and liquids can be transformed into "solid" objects. When energy conversion takes place that which was invisible and intangible can become both visible and tangible—"solid."

The paraphysical explanation for UFOs involves the fact that these vehicles and even their occupants can actually be caused to assume physical or solid form, visible to human eyes, but are also capable of being invisible, according to the visual frequency adopted at a particular time.

If the phenomenon basically consists of energy rather than "solid" matter, it would necessarily be invisible to humans. However, by manipulating patterns of frequency any "earthly" shape can be assumed, from monsters to midgets, to mother-ships in the sky. For their movements and maneuverability it seems they utilize electromagnetic principles, with amazing flexibility. The fact of their being paraphysical apparently does not rule out their use of physical laws, including electromagnetism.

Physicists tell us that what we think of as reality is in fact an illusion, and that matter really consists of confined energy. Moving electrons, together with energy particles, actually form the atoms all around us, varying in weight and density as they do. Atoms are joined to become molecules, which then have specific shapes and sizes. If we could be reduced to the size of an atom we would find there was a fantastic amount of space all around us. What we think of as "solid" results from confining the molecules in a specific way, and the molecules making up that substance can be changed to take another form. A log of wood is entirely solid, and we cannot put our hands through it, but if we put it on a fire soon the molecules change their combination, and we can put our hands through the resultant smoke. The molecules are not then combined in a solid form as we think of solid, but by the application of fire those molecules have become farther apart. Molecules can be changed by many processes such as heat, or even by physical reshaping with implements such as axes, saws, and hammers. We are able to manipulate energy, and to adjust the shapes in which molecules are "held" together.

Our concepts of reality depend to a great extent on what comes within the grasp of our immediate senses, but in fact we are surrounded by electromagnetic waves of various types, of which we are usually unaware. If we zero in on one and listen to a radio broadcast we fully accept that that particular radio frequency is real. There are dozens of others all around us, just as real, but beyond our specific comprehension at a particular moment of time.

About Frequencies and Vibrations

So far much that we have said on these subjects would not be objected to by most people, for they know that the marvels of science show that these things are indeed true. However, as we proceed with the subject we quickly enter a realm where people are not so ready to nod their heads and agree, partly because they do not understand. Discussion fairly quickly merges into the occult, and we touch areas known through the centuries to spiritists with their auras, frequencies, and vibrations. Those who accept these concepts have no problem in accepting that there are other planes of existence, with spirit beings all around us, even though we are unaware of them.

We repeat, some of the concepts involved with the study of the UFO phenomenon are so unusual and different from the normal experiences of most people, that in this volume we deliberately quote others who have written. It is frankly confessed that part of the reason for this is to let it be seen that some of these ideas are not simply the wild mental aberrations of this author. John Keel discusses the world of illusion, and makes this statement:[9]

> Although you can't see it, your body is surrounded by self-generated fields of radiation. The occultists have always called this radiation the aura. There have been many people—mediums and sensitives—who have claimed that they could actually see this human aura. Some amazing demonstrations and tests have been performed before large groups of witnesses in which sensitives were able to look at a stranger's aura, and were supposedly noticing various shadings in that aura, so that they could accurately announce, "You have a scar on your abdomen, and there's a black cloud over your liver. You've been having liver trouble." Special eye glasses have been on the market for years so that almost anyone could see the aura. Since the human body does radiate infrared, the glasses do work!

In recent years scientists have begun to take the concept of the aura seriously. The Albert Einstein Medical Center in Philadelphia has been conducting experiments with infrared devices for some time, and their results have been surprising. Tumors and other disorders show up in these thermogram photos and "These studies have confirmed the wild claims of the occult aura watchers."[10]

Similar experiments have been conducted with an ultrasound system, especially by the Bio-Medical Engineering Center at Northwestern University, at the university's Technological Institute—"A spot of defective welding appears in varying colors, while good weld is uniform."[11]

In that same context, Keel discusses in some detail specific examples that fitted into the observed colors associated with the UFO phenomenon, and even the sound used by UFOs.

He makes this conclusion:[12]

> All of these events seem to prove that a large part of the UFO phenomenon is hidden from us and is taking place beyond the limited range of our eyes. We can only see the objects and the entities under certain circumstances, and *perhaps only certain types of people can see them at all.*
>
> Thus, by all the standards of our sciences (and our common sense), the UFOs do not really exist as solid objects. They may be a constant part of our environment, but they are not an actual part of our reality. We cannot, therefore, catalog them as manufactured products of some extraterrestrial civilization sharing our own dimensions of time and space. They are extradimensional, able to move through our spatial coordinates at will but also able to enter and leave our three-dimensional world. If this is a true hypothesis, then they may also be operating beyond the limitations of our time coordinates. Our years may be minutes to them. Our future may be their past, and thus they have total knowledge of the things in store for us.

On Manipulating Objects of Earth

These observations by Keel are not wild conjectures. We have seen that he used convincing evidence, based on extensive investigation, to show that there is a color system associated with UFOs. He suggests that as UFOs and their occupants move into our spatial and time coordinates, they slow down, as it were, from higher frequencies, passing progressively through ultraviolet, violet, bluish green, and then, if they stabilize within our dimensions, they become a glaring white as they radiate energy on all frequencies. With radical maneuverings at high speeds, frequencies are altered, and so the colors also change. Keel shows that in the majority of landing reports the UFOs were said to have turned orange or red before they descended, then solidified when they settled to the ground and so the light would dim or go out altogether. When they took off, they again began to glow red, and it would depend on their subsequent movements as to the colors seen by the witnesses.

Keel's argument is that these objects have been manipulated so that they temporarily simulate terrestrial matter. Such theories are no longer regarded as superstition or magic. We live in an age when it is being scientifically demonstrated that even metal spoons can be bent by mental power—even by two teen-agers who found they had the same power of "mind over matter" which they had seen demonstrated on television. It is interesting to mention in passing that the mental powers and observed results of the "pupils" have not been challenged as those of the "master" spoon-bender have been! It is recognized today that there are energy forces that are at times utilized, forces not so recognized even a century ago, except possibly as demon possession.

Today there are universities and institutions of higher learning with departments investigating paraphysical phenomena. Duke University in North Carolina, the Cambridge University in England, and an institution in Leningrad in the USSR are all known to have highly qualified science personnel conducting research into such concepts as extrasensory perception, telepathy, and other paranormal activities.[18]

There is good reason to suggest the paraphysical explanation for many UFO sightings. Some who do not fully subscribe to that hypothesis still see border areas of possible agreement—areas where the physical and the paraphysical might be brought together.

That spirit of inquiry has been increased in the 1980s by the fantastic revelation of so much previously secret information.

Is Teleportation Feasible?

Some scientists even believe that teleportation is not entirely unthinkable. They seriously suggest the possibility of the energy in a series of atoms being converted into a beam that could be transmitted to a distant point, perhaps even at the speed of light, and then be reconstructed in its original form. Today this is still a way-out concept, but in UFO literature and in other records of the past there do appear to be cases which defy explanation, where people have apparently been transported thousands of miles in a moment of time. It is possible that much of this can be attributed to hallucination, or delusion, for some cases are undoubtedly hoaxes. However, as with so many aspects of these strange phenomena, the wise shaking of the head does not give all the answer. The evidence is convincing that powers outside humans can control both mind and body, and also manipulate persons, in ways that are sometimes beyond the intent of the individual concerned.

Brinsley Le Poer Trench discusses some of these cases of apparent teleportation, and then elaborates about some of the occupants of UFOs. He—along with other ufologists—suggests that these occupants can flash their light beam back toward their UFO and then use that beam to enter the vehicle. This sounds incredible, and even crazy, but as our earth-bound scientists are beginning to suggest the same sort of possibilities for teleportation, it would be entirely possible for the concept to be known to intelligent beings possessing knowledge greater than that of humans. Trench has this relevant comment:[14]

There are, incidentally, many other cases on record of entities coming down and going back to UFOs on light beams.

Ufologists who write seriously about teleportation having taken place in modern times often quote Ivan

Sanderson. He started research on the subject when he could not explain how huge queen ants of the mound-building variety inexplicably vanished from their nests and then would suddenly appear in another nest miles away. There are quite a number of other stories—such as that concerning people traveling together, driving along a highway, their cars following each other, when a mist came behind the first car. When the mist cleared away only moments later, the second car had disappeared. Two days later a telephone call told how the car with its occupants was in Mexico, 4,000 miles away from where the incident took place.[15]

There are other similar stories. Perhaps the most uncanny—and probably incredible—relates to a navy destroyer that is supposed to have suddenly disappeared from the Philadelphia navy yards, then appeared in Newport News in Virginia, and finally reappeared back at the Philadelphia yards. This story comes out in *The Allende Letters* which Dr. M. K. Jessup purportedly received in 1959.[16] We repeat, it is probably not to be taken seriously, though sincerely believed by those whose names were linked with the story.

This is one of those seemingly incredible stories associated with this whole subject, but if there is deception, once again it is possibly the original narrator who is deceived rather than being a deliberate deceiver himself. Certainly one would expect this incident to be more widely known through relatives if it "really" happened.

Carlos Allende is supposed to have written these Allende Letters, and he talks about the personnel involved having become temporarily invisible, with some being insane when the project ended. Allende claimed that he could make a very real contribution to the success of teleportation and invisibility, which would give the United States Navy a tremendous advantage over other earth powers.

Some writers who discuss the possibility of teleportation suggest that something approaching a primitive form of this is in operation every time a telephone is used. As a man speaks into the telephone, the electricity in that instrument vibrates at a specific frequency. A metal plate at the other end, a diaphragm, responds to a magnet, and vibrates at that same frequency, and in doing this it duplicates the voice. Thus a man can speak in Australia and be heard immediately in New York, or in some distant part of the earth's surface where there is a telephone link. There need not even be wires, for it can be achieved by radio connection. As we have said, some ufologists suggest that in a sense this is a primitive form of teleportation.

We saw that there are even those who suggest that telephones are being used in ways that cannot be attributed to human intervention. Highly complicated equipment is needed to tamper with telephone calls, and it is seriously suggested that nonhuman forces are exploiting these principles and interfering with telephones and telephone calls. There have been literally thousands of reports of UFOs hovering over microwave relay towers utilized by telephone companies.

These possibilities of strange activities are not discussed only by "cranks." In our discussion as to the possibility of UFOs being associated with paraphysical phenomena, we quoted RAF Air Marshal Sir Victor Goddard. In that same address, Sir Victor Goddard went on to make this statement:[17]

> The astral world of illusion, which (on physical evidence) is greatly inhabited by illusion-prone spirits, is well known for its multifarious imaginative activities and exultations. Similarly some of its denizens are eager to exemplify principalities and powers. Others pronounce upon morality, spirituality, deity, etc. All of these astral exponents who invoke human consciousness may be sincere, but many of their theses may be framed to propagate some special phantom, perhaps of an earlier incarnation, or to indulge an inveterate and continuing technological urge toward materialistic progress, or simply to astonish and disturb the gullible for the devil of it.

"A Staggering Cosmic Put-On"

John Keel suggests that Sir Victor's remarks are even harder to believe than the claims of various UFO cults. As he discusses the import of Sir Victor's comments, Keel himself states:[18]

In essence, he means that the UFO phenomenon is actually a staggering cosmic put-on; a joke perpetrated by invisible entities who have always delighted in frightening, confusing, and misleading the human race. The activities of these entities have been carefully recorded throughout history, and we will be leaning heavily on those historical records in this book.

Keel does lean heavily on historical records—his book is very well documented, and he himself makes the point that he selects those cases that appear to be most acceptable. Another authoritative work to which he refers is a publication compiled by the U.S. Library of Congress for the Air Force Office of Scientific Research, entitled *UFOs and Related Subjects: An Annotated Bibliography*. He quotes from Miss Lyn E. Catoe, a senior bibliographer who had read thousands of UFO articles, books, and publications. He quotes from her preface to this 400-page book:[19]

A large part of the available UFO literature is closely linked with mysticism and the metaphysical. It deals with subjects like mental telepathy, automatic writing, and invisible entities, as well as phenomena like poltergeist manifestations and possession.... Many of the UFO reports now being published in the popular press recount alleged incidents that are strikingly similar to demoniac possession and psychic phenomena which has long been known to theologians and parapsychologists.

How Should UFO Investigations Continue?

Because of the conclusion toward which this present book is leading, the views of one other authority obviously should be considered in this study of UFO phenomena. We refer to Dr. Edward U. Condon, who headed the University of Colorado's study on UFOs that the U.S. government funded, to which we have already referred. He caused a furor among many in UFO circles by his insistence that the scientific team involved in this project had found no evidence that UFOs originated from outside the earth, or that there had been any serious censorship of UFO sightings and contacts on the part of the U.S. government. One of Dr. Condon's conclusions was that there was no point in continuing the investigation of UFOs along the lines followed in previous years, but rather, if there was to be further investigation, it should be directed along other lines instead of the mere interviewing of people who have seen something peculiar.

John Keel has tended to back Dr. Condon's assessment, and Keel has put his point remarkably clearly. Those who are seriously interested in the subject should read Keel's book, *UFOs ... Operation Trojan Horse.* The unbiased reader will find it of real interest and value. Even though his conclusions have often gone against deeply held views of many ufologists, his arguments are respected. He suggests that the real UFO story must encompass more than the actual manifestations that are being observed around the world, for ghosts and phantoms and mental aberrations are also relevant—that invisible world that surrounds us and occasionally even engulfs us. He urges that we should seriously consider the influence of "a world of illusion and hallucination, where the unreal seems very real, and where reality itself is distorted by strange forces which can seemingly manipulate space, time, and physical matter—forces which are almost entirely beyond our powers of comprehension."[20]

In that same context he says that scientists who have given up the study of UFOs have not been silenced by the air force or the CIA, but were rendered mute by the awesome and overwhelming realization that man is not alone, that the human race is merely a trifling part of something much bigger.

Keel suggests that sometimes these UFO "visitors" are hostile, at other times mischievous, and at other times apparently friendly. He points out that the manifestations range from childish mischief to acts of horrifying destruction; that sometimes the phenomenon has driven people mad but at other times it had produced remarkable cures. He says there are well-documented events in which the mysterious objects and enterprising occupants have actually interceded directly in human affairs and thereby they have thwarted disaster.

At that point we suggest, with all due respect to John Keel, that it is also possible that the apparently friendly acts of these beings are of the same character as the minor prophecies which they give from time to time—it is possible that they are merely baits to gain the confidence of a wide circle who are thereby duped.

As though to explain the reason behind his fascinating subtitle, "Operation Trojan Horse," Keel begins to bring that part of his section to a close as follows:[21]

> Many flying saucers seem to be nothing more than a disguise for some hidden phenomenon. They are like trojan horses descending into our forests and farm fields, promising salvation and offering us the splendor of some great super civilization in the sky. While the statuesque long-haired "Venusians" have been chatting benignly with isolated traveling salesmen and farm wives, a multitude of shimmering lights and metallic disks have been silently busying themselves in the forests of Canada, the outback country of Australia, and the swamps of Michigan.

The conclusions to be drawn from such observations are in some ways frightening if one is prepared to consider seriously the possibility of paraphysical phenomena sharing our air space. They are frightening too because of the very real possibility that these vehicles and their occupants involve spiritual powers. Such conclusions are rejected by many people, either because of the personal commitment that this could demand, or because of the possibility of ridicule.

However, what is the alternative? It is undoubtedly true that the great majority of sightings have been of nonsolid objects—reliable sightings of solid metallic objects have been relatively rare. According to John Keel, referring to these so-called soft (nonsolid) sightings, "The scope, frequency, and distribution of the sightings make the popular extraterrestrial (interplanetary) hypothesis completely untenable."[22]

Even apart from the paraphysical and spiritual concepts, the UFO phenomenon cannot be studied as many other scientific phenomena can be studied, for it is beyond experimental control. In the main, visits by UFOs are unscheduled as far as earthlings can know in advance, and the observers are not necessarily competent to make a scientific analysis of a totally unexpected happening.

The evidence accumulates, but in the meantime many scientists still have an open mind. Even among those who have come from being out-and-out skeptics, now to identify themselves as moving in the direction of those who firmly believe in UFOs, there are many unresolved questions. As Dr. Hynek states, "After more than twenty years' association with the problem, I still have few answers and no viable hypothesis."[23]

Reports of sightings should still be taken seriously, for, as Dr. Hynek states, "The part we ignore . . . may contain the clue to the whole subject."[24]

Is that clue in the realm of spirits and demons? To that we now turn.

Chapter 13

Vampires and UFOs

The vampire is renowned in mythology for its blood-sucking from humans, and there is the serious possibility that UFOs also are veritable life-suckers from humans. Limited as to their power to appear in tangible form, they temporarily utilize the bodies of men and women, boys and girls, and even animals, to aid their transmogrification into humanoid or monster form.

There are many pointers to this, for it seems that when these beings enter the solid state which is necessary for humans to observe them, they utilize atoms from the world in which we live. Some ufologists even claim that this is also true for UFOs themselves, and that earth's "material" substances are necessary for the "manufacture" of these vehicles: and that this is the explanation for disappearing airplanes, and the draining of energy from power stations, power lines, and automobiles. It seems that they do actually take blood and other physical matter from human beings and animals alike. The theory is that in this way they are able to adapt themselves so that we limited humans will understand them, and ultimately be programmed by them.

Another frightening occurrence is where the UFO occupant is supposed to have aimed a cubelike weapon toward the contactee, and a paralytic state followed, lasting until the UFO took off and disappeared. Some parapsychologists suggest that this akinesia is actually part of the reason for the occupant of the spacecraft materializing—that the being is actually brought into material, visible form by utilizing energy drawn from the contactee himself, resulting in his temporary paralysis.[1]

Psychic Projections?

Other investigators of the UFO phenomenon have suggested that the witnesses have been involved with some sort of psychic projection, though this does not make the experience any the less real. Over and over again it seems that attributes of life are "borrowed" by these nonearthly beings for their own purposes, even though it is for a brief time only. There have been many cases of temporary paralysis, of children in trancelike states, even of some animals being completely drained of their blood, and of other physical matter associated with earthly life being utilized.

Even the stories with sexual overtones might be in the same category. There are a number of seemingly genuine incidents where some attempt was made to take human life potential by sexual contact—not always by the sex act itself. It is true that fact and fiction merge in some of these "incidents," and that some experiences have been grossly exaggerated. However, the similarity of many reports indicates the genuineness of at least some of them.

John Keel theorizes as to how beings can materialize at séances, and also as UFO occupants. He states:[2]

In order to materialize and take on definite form, these entities seem to require a source of energy; a fire or a living thing—a plant, a tree, a human medium (or contactee). Our sciences have not reached a point where they can offer us any kind of working hypothesis for this process. But we can speculate that these beings need living energy which they can restructure into a physical form. Perhaps that is why dogs and animals tend to vanish in flap areas. Perhaps the living cells of those animals are somehow used by the ultraterrestrials to create forms which we can see and sense with our limited perceptions. Perhaps human and animal blood is also essential for this process.

Incredible? Yet it makes sense. Why are UFOs so often involved with power lines, and even with atomic plants? Why do so many contactees report that their car was temporarily stalled, with electric apparatus suddenly dead? Is it because there is a point beyond which these entities cannot go unless "earth" life forces are available to them? Is that the reason for their many incursions into the sea, to extract yet other forms of energy or life?

Perhaps the same physical life principle is seen in the New Testament incident where Jesus healed a man possessed of many demons, demons who gave their name as "Legion." In the New Testament record, those demons asked for and were given permission to enter a herd of swine nearby. The herd of swine then raced down the slope and drowned in the lake—almost as though they knew they were occupied by totally objectionable creatures.

It is possible that these demon creatures are unable to produce life—we know from the words of the Lord Jesus that the angels neither marry nor are given in marriage. Some scholars believe that the Bible verse in Genesis that the "sons of God saw the daughters of men that they were fair, and took wives of whom they would," means that demons had sexual relations with women. Others believe that "the sons of God" were men of the godly line of Seth, while "the daughters of men" were descended from Cain who had murdered his brother Abel.

Some argue that the terminology used about "taking wives" means that they literally married them—that it was not simply a case of isolated sex acts. We cannot be dogmatic on the issue, because scholars disagree. However, it is this author's belief that only God can give life, He being the very source of life. Thus it would seem entirely possible that there is a limitation to the powers of these beings, and that the only new life available to them is whatever they can "borrow," whether it be human, animal, or even energy forces such as electricity.

Hypnosis and Paralysis

We have referred to contactees who suffered temporary paralysis, and there have been many other health effects following contact with the occupants of these strange craft. Some people appear to have been hypnotized, with instructions to forget all that had happened. Elsewhere we refer to Mr. and Mrs. Barney Hill, who "recovered" the time "lost," and the details of their experience, only under hypnosis. How many others have undergone UFO hypnotism and now have no memory of it?

There are many indications that very large numbers of people have had some sort of contact with UFOs. In *The True Report on Flying Saucers*, a Gallup Poll report for 1966 states that over 5 million Americans believed they had seen a flying saucer, and that about 50 million Americans believed that phenomena regularly reported were "real" and not figments of the imagination. Computerized results have caused many top scientists to realize that, whatever UFOs are, they are a very real phenomenon.

Otto Binder discusses the great numbers of sightings around the world, then has an interesting statement:[3]

At any rate, it would seem that the expanding series of saucer sightings in waves, from 1964 to date, is all building up to a crescendo, as if the saucer men are conditioning earth people to seeing saucers, and gradually forcing even the most recalcitrant scientists and government authorities to realize the sightings are not figments of imagination, but real.

Not only have many seen UFOs, but there is also a growing army of those who claim to have had actual contact with UFO occupants. An authoritative, and possibly conservative, estimate is that there are 50,000 silent contactees in the United States alone.[4]

It could well be there are thousands of people who

do have information and are not prepared to reveal it because of threatened consequences to themselves. Possibly many do not know they have that "knowledge" because they themselves gained it in a hypnotic state.

Hypnotized Slaves Await the Signal

Nations could be conquered by the infiltration of agents into government seats of authority, and it is surely more frightening to think that mankind could be overcome and even destroyed by programmed men and women from within their own ranks. If there is indeed a final confrontation approaching, an army of people could be involved. They could be ready to take action which they themselves do not even anticipate, but yet with no option but to obey when the prearranged signal is given. Their reaction would be as those under hypnosis—they would obey because they have been conditioned to obey, at a given signal.

We are not alone in suggesting this dreadful possibility. To quote John Keel once again:[5]

> We have no way of knowing how many human beings throughout the world may have been processed in this manner, since they would have absolutely no memory of undergoing the experience, and so we have no way of determining who among us has strange and sinister "programs" lying dormant in the dark corners of his mind.
> Suppose a plan is to process millions of people and then at some future date trigger all of those minds at one time? Would we suddenly have a world of saints? Or would we have a world of armed maniacs shooting at one another from bell towers?

If Armageddon, to which the Bible points, is indeed a final battle in which human and nonhuman forces alike wage that dreadful conflict to the death, this sort of "programming" is a real possibility, and it appears to be proceeding at breakneck speed across the whole of the world. It is reported that the term "Armageddon" has been used in a message to a contactee[6] and other "end of the world" messages have been given. Is there a desperate preparation for a last-ditch stand by the forces of evil, a final attempt to thwart the plans of the Holy God against Whom they have rebelled? Bible history gives many examples where Satanic forces have attempted completely to destroy God's plans that would result in total blessings for man. There has continually been a diabolical scheme of bending minds by deceitful assurances and "brainwashing." Post-hypnotic suggestions, with in-built commands for action to be triggered at a given signal, would fit the general pattern of rebellion consistently seen in the Bible records.

A Frightening Prospect

The prospect is frightening. It is entirely possible that by post-hypnotic suggestion a whole army of people could suddenly find themselves willing slaves to intelligent beings who would care nothing for the welfare of those slaves, or of the world itself as we know it. If there is some great super-plan of a spiritual counterattack to reach its culmination in Armageddon, it could well be that that army of slaves will be available to obey orders, without even knowing beforehand that they have been inducted into the armed forces of what the Bible refers to as principalities and powers.

The indications are that even children are at times utilized for the implementation of the plans of these evil powers. That possibility is illustrated by the following incident.

On December 12, 1967, Mrs. Rita Malley was driving along a public highway to her home at Ithaca, New York, with her five-year-old son Dana in the back seat of her vehicle. At about 7:00 P.M. she suddenly realized that a red light was apparently following her, and as she was moving at slightly above the speed level, her first reaction was that she was about to be pulled over. She looked through her window and found that it was not a police car behind her but an eerie flying object, moving along above the power lines at the left of her car. Then she found she no longer had control of her vehicle, and shouted to her son to brace himself. However, he remained motionless as though he were in a trance.[7]

A white beam of light flashed down from the vehicle overhead, then she heard voices that sounded weird, broken, and jerky. She herself became hysterical, but through it all her son took no notice whatever of her cries. The radio was not on, but she heard those voices tell her that at that moment a friend of hers had been involved in a terrible accident some miles away. The next day she found that this was indeed true. The voices also told her that her son would not remember anything that had happened. The ordeal was terrifying to Mrs. Malley herself, and for some time afterward whenever she remembered the episode she would break down sobbing.

What part did her five-year-old son have in this episode? Was there some way in which his body was utilized? Were there limitations on the powers of these beings and they needed a human as a medium through whom they could operate? Some UFO writers state seriously that young children are pliable, and as they have not developed the fixed attitudes and prejudices typical of older people, they are ideal for the purposes of these "space visitors." Whether they are space visitors or not, it may very well be that this conclusion is close to the awful truth. Keel points out that a large percentage of these events seem to occur when a small child is present, and that in this case of Dana Malley, he himself went into a trance. Many such trances have been reported.[8]

It would seem possible, then, that pliable children are especially useful for the purposes of these beings. Many children have been used as tools so that men and women would believe in these beings who have a plan whose totality has not yet been revealed.

If the above incident were just the story of one

woman, it could be put aside with a question mark alongside it. However, there are so many of these incidents—not only with children—that the total picture becomes alarming. These beings did indeed know that a specific person some distance away was involved right then in an accident; over and over again there is evidence that UFO occupants have a great knowledge about individual contactees, and even have some knowledge of future events. However, as we have seen, there is very good reason to believe that either their knowledge of future events is limited, or that they deliberately deceive as to major events.

These incidents are not limited to children. Mrs. Ralph Butler was watching flashing lights outside Owatonna in Minnesota one night in November, 1966.[9] She was with a friend, and suddenly her friend became immobile, with her head dipped down. Mrs. Butler herself heard a voice talking to her, but soon the ordeal was over. However, when the two friends tried to discuss the incident later, both found they immediately suffered blinding headaches. Mrs. Butler also told of hearing strange voices on her radio, and of having peculiar visits from "air force officers." This pattern is reported by many who claim to have been contacted by UFO personnel.

The Butler family have experienced various poltergeist phenomena since that 1966 experience—glass objects moving around and breaking without any known cause, strange noises being heard throughout the house, even telephones and television sets being strangely interfered with.

This sort of activity has followed many other supposed saucer sightings. The similarities between the stories are of such a nature as to cause surprise at first—someone temporarily in a trance, men posing as air force or other officials, those men being slight in stature with dark olive skins and pointed features, and the contactees having dreadful headaches, hallucinations, and nightmares. Some of them have gone into trances and have temporarily become mediums through whom strange voices could be heard.

It Is No Longer Amusing

Many such incidents that ten years ago would have caused many readers to smile are now taken seriously. Even though a great majority of the population will only "believe what they can see," there is no longer the widespread amused skepticism and ridicule that was associated with stories of UFOs even a decade ago.

Perhaps Mrs. Butler's friend was especially suited for this incident in which she unwittingly found herself. As John Keel states:.[10]

> The UFO phenomenon seems to be largely subjective; that is, specific kinds of people become involved and are actually manipulated by the phenomenon in the same way that it manipulates matter. These subjective experiences are far more important to our study than the random, superficial sightings.

Another contactee story is that of Helio Aguiar, a statistician employed by a bank in Bahia, Brazil. On April 24, 1959, he claims he saw a silvery disk, and on top of the disk itself was a dome with windows. He saw certain symbols on the underside of the object, and took some photographs. His story to a Brazilian journalist, Joao Martins, told of what happened after that:[11]

> He began to feel pressure on his brain, and a state of progressive confusion overtook him. He felt vaguely as though he were being ordered by somebody to write something down. It was as though he were being hypnotized. As he was winding the film on before proceeding to take a fourth picture, he lost all sense of what was happening.

According to the report, when Helio Aguiar came to, he had a piece of paper in his hand, with a message in his own handwriting. The message was:[12]

Put an absolute stop to all atomic tests for warlike purposes. The balance of the universe is threatened. We shall remain vigilant and ready to intervene.

The expression "the balance of the universe" occurs very often in the messages of the supposed contactees—individuals who could not have known of each other or of the messages that have been given to other people all around the world.

Keel states that in 1963 comedian Red Skelton had a strange experience of lapsing into a semitrance for about an hour. When he regained full consciousness, he found a terrifying message in his notebook—he has no memory of writing it or thinking the words. The message was: "President Kennedy will be killed in November."[13]

What causes this strange intrusion into a man's personal consciousness? Why do so many "contactees" suffer from exhaustion, blinding headaches, and depression? How are the similarities to spiritism and séances explained if they are not in the same category? What answers can be given in terms of psychological concepts?

It is difficult to know just where the paraphysical, the physical, and other phenomena merge. It is believed that about one third of the earth's population are capable of at least some measure of "extrasensory perception," and that others can be "tuned in" to this sort of experience by direct assocation with those who have such special capacities. This is the sort of thing that happens when less sensitive human beings make contact with evil forces through a medium.

Researchers have shown that even plants respond to sympathetic treatment, and have some sort of awareness when other nearby plants are deliberately injured. "Sympathy pains" are at times experienced by men whose wives are undergoing labor pains, with correlations even from a distance. It is not enough to smile and write off these experiences as simply "psychological," whatever that might mean, when someone makes such a glib diagnosis. There are strange interrelationships of human and other emotions, including pain, pointing to relationships of energy patterns which a century ago would probably have been ridiculed. In the 1970s these concepts are not ridiculed, for many strange things have happened. There have been so many proven events that a generation ago would have been regarded as the distorted wanderings of unbalanced people, that we are now much more ready to accept the fantastic as the commonplace.

UFOs and Spiritism

That energy source is possibly part of the explanation for materializations at séances. Many of those materializations have actually been photographed. Though there have been many fakes and much trickery, it is certainly true that some materializations are genuine, though temporary in nature. They do not always appear in dark rooms, with trickery possible, but at times they are seen in fully lighted rooms, totally surrounded by flesh-and-blood witnesses. It seems there are similar paraphysical explanations for both séance materializations and the "materializations" of UFOs and their occupants.

In fact, there are many similarities between spiritism and the manifestations of UFOs. Paraphysical explanations are given to explain "elementals" at séances, beings supposedly conjured up by secret magical rites whereby the form of either a beautiful woman or of a hideous monster can be as easily presented. It would seem that such a being could be formed, virtually mindless, and without a body. It would stay in a specific center and merely repeat whatever it was instructed to do—over great periods of time, possibly even centuries.

Certain rites can at times cause the power to be "dissolved." There is much evidence from many parts of the world that the Christian practice of casting out demons is very real, and is not a superstitious carry-over from ancient times. The exorcism of evil spirits, sometimes undertaken by Christian ministers, can indeed be effective. Through the power of Christ the Christian is "in touch" with a Power greater than any demonic force. The practicing Christian can claim that power—he need not fear demons. Jesus gave His disciples power over all evil spirits. This is not meant to endorse the exhibitionism that is supposedly carried on in the name of Christ.

Sometimes it is difficult to know what form of paraphysical activity is involved—so-called spiritism or UFOs. The evidence indicates that they are really the same phenomena. We saw that many of the contactees have experienced akinesia—immobility—and this has not been restricted to sightings of a UFO in a field or near a highway. Numbers of cases have been reported where someone has awakened to see an intruder in his bedroom, then a warning or a message has been given. After that, the intruder has disappeared, and the contactee's immobility has ended. Some will argue that this is what is called a hypnopompic phenomenon whereby a dream continues on into the state of wakefulness. However, it has happened very often, and such a solution is not convincing in all cases.

Levitation is another well-known phenomenon associated with séances and mediums, and it is at times associated with UFOs. One case dates to November, 1953, when James Greer was supposed to have been levitated into the sky. His brother Albert and a hired hand were with him on the farm near Zanesville in Ohio, and Albert actually grabbed at his brother's legs as he rose, but watched in horror—so the report goes—as James vanished into the sky. Then they saw a blinding flash that sped off to the northeast—a description highly reminiscent of many UFO sightings.[14]

This is another indication that the paraphysical solution cannot be ruled out with UFOs, and that there is a very real possibility that UFOs and spiritism are linked.

In the 1980s we are much more ready to accept such a possibility or at least to open our minds to consider it.

Modern Beginnings

Modern spiritism began in March, 1848, with Kate and Margaret Fox, aged twelve and fifteen respectively. They heard mysterious rappings on the wall of their house in Hydesville, New York, and soon found they could communicate with a spirit. They developed a system of yes/no answers, and a code for the letters of the alphabet, and then they carried out conversations with their unseen visitor. They found they could communicate in other places besides Hydesville, and so they held séances in various other towns.

It is interesting to conjecture that possibly the geographic location itself had some importance. Before the Fox family moved into that house, it had been occupied by the family of Mitchell Weekman. They were worried by mysterious knockings on the door, with nobody there. Then a member of the family—an eight-year-old girl—screamed out that a cold, invisible hand was caressing her body. The Weekmans moved out and the Fox family moved in. Apparently the spirit-visitor was prepared to communicate with whoever was available in that particular area.

John Keel makes the point that this was only a few miles from Joseph Smith's former home in Wayne County and he comments:[15]

So here is another freakish coincidence to ponder: Both Mormonism and spiritualism were born in the same county in places only a few miles from each other!

Spiritism became a popular "hobby" in the following decades, and, though many of the mediums were shown to be fraudulent, there were others who undertook feats that were beyond normal explanations. There are well-known names associated with spiritism, perhaps the best being Sir Arthur Conan Doyle who created "Sherlock Holmes."

Investigations in depth of the spiritist phenomena conclude that these entities use their knowledge of individuals to convince them of the existence of a spirit world. However, they give only enough information to suggest their own greater intelligence and power. Thus they seek to ensure the obedience of mere mortals to themselves.

There is disturbing evidence that these nonterrestrial beings care little about the earthlings whom they use. One of the best-known examples is that of Reverend Arthur Ford who was the special instrument of a spirit called "Fletcher." Typical of the sort of information he could give was the message he relayed for the widow of Harry Houdini, in a code used by the Houdinis in one of their mind-reading acts. The code was unknown to any but the couple themselves. Mrs. Houdini confirmed that the message could only come from her husband. If we accept the genuineness of the report, this is another indication of the knowledge these spirit beings have about men and women of flesh and blood.

Human Beings "Possessed"

Reverend Ford traveled extensively, conducting séances all over the United States. Despite the fact that he made himself so constantly available to this spirit who called himself "Fletcher," the spirit apparently had no interest in Ford's personal health except as it was important for Ford to be fit enough to continue as a medium through whom it could express itself. Ruth Montgomery, author and Washington reporter, was asking advice while Ford was in a trance. Mrs. Montgomery stated that "Fletcher" had seemed totally disinterested in the problems which Ford himself was facing at that time, and she asked if he should undergo a medical checkup. "Fletcher" is supposed to have snapped, "He'd better do something. If he doesn't, I can't work through him much longer."[16]

Although Ford had made himself available to "Fletcher" for nearly half a century, "Fletcher" was completely disinterested in his problems and his welfare. These entities want only to communicate, and have no desire for any personal involvement that would be to the advantage of those through whom or to whom they are communicating.

It is also established that these beings reveal intimate details of the life histories of their victims—details "which least of all they wished others either to hear or know."[17]

At other times these beings who "possess" human beings will speak intelligently—sometimes using obscenities—in foreign tongues, even correcting the grammar of those testing the reality of the experience.[18] In passing, it is relevant to mention that this is a counterfeit of a similar experience to which the Apostle Paul refers in his first letter to the Corinthians, chapters 13 and 14. Satanic forces have always attempted to imitate Divine realities.

Earlier we referred to visits and messages from Mr. Ashtar, and also from "the Queen of Heaven." Both men and women have been involved—as in times of old, both with visions and actual contacts.

Similar appearances, supposedly from "the Queen of the Universe," have taken place in recent times. Very often young girls are the ones who first report the visions, and there are a significant number of cases involving young girls with UFOs as well as visions and miracles.[19] Often there is evidence that hypnotism has been involved. After initial experiences that excited them, the girls have gone into trances which at times would last for hours. They themselves remained immobile, in strange kneeling positions, their heads thrown back, and totally oblivious to all the people around them as they stared at the vision.

It is even possible that these nonhuman entities do not even possess individuality in the human sense. It is possible that some greater power is able to manipulate the human mind, and that "this mental (and also emotional) manipulation is the key to our mystery."[20] Many of those who have been contacted by UFOs display the same symptoms that have been demonstrated by "possessed" people at spiritual séances, etc. It is all too true that human beings can be exposed to some outside force that can insert information into the mind—a truly fearsome programming.

We have seen that many of those who have been contacted or in various ways have been involved with UFOs have suffered medical effects. Often this is not only exterior (as with marks of burning, etc.), but there have been very real mental problems. At times the outside entity is utilizing the contactee, especially when children are involved, so that "some powerful beam of electromagnetic energy is broadcast into that mind, by-passing the biological sensory channels."[21]

The fearful consequences to the individual who has been subjected to this treatment are obvious. It is a sad commentary that the drastic effects of drugs such as LSD are thoroughly realized, but some of the effects to which we have referred, associated as they are with spiritism and UFOs, are not recognized by very many.

Not Mental Aberrations

There is the tendency to regard UFOs as the mental aberrations of crackpots who see flying saucers in every second tree. However, the danger is in fact very real, and widely spread. It goes beyond national and cultural boundaries, and certainly is not limited to "mental cases." In fact, the point is made in UFO writings from time to time that UFO contacts are not claimed by mentally deranged persons: if contacts resulted from mental aberrations, one would expect that many in "mental institutions" would report such experiences, but this has not proved to be the case. The contactees are normally healthy persons as far as mentality is concerned. Mental problems develop after, not before, the UFO contact.

There is even reason to believe that some of the same contacts and messages can be traced to drug addiction as can be traced to contacts with UFOs, and the same pattern has been shown also through Ouija boards and séances. The principalities and powers, against whom the Apostle Paul warned, are very active.

Throughout this manuscript it has become clear that we are suggesting the possibility of demon activity: it is at least a major part of the answer to the UFO phenomenon. The utilization of paraphysical phenomena has been practiced by demon forces through the centuries.

Such talk, of course, will turn many off. Some who live in "Western" cultures are quite unprepared to think of the possibility of such things as demons, but that does not alter the reality of the phenomenon, for:[22]

> Demonology is not just another crackpot-ology. It is the ancient and scholarly study of the monsters and demons who have seemingly coexisted wtth man throughout history.... The manifestations and occurrences described in this imposing literature are similar, if not entirely identical, to the UFO phenomenon itself. Victims of demonomania [possession] suffer the very same medical and emotional symptoms as the UFO contactees. Demonomania is so common that it has spawned the minor medical and psychiatric study of demonopathy.

As we say, many will reject this conclusion because to them demons are a totally unacceptable concept. Others are convinced that the answer to the UFO phenomenon is to be found in the electromagnetism theory.

Despite the fact that many academics reject the possibility of demonology, it should be stated that there is much literature on this subject that comes from highly educated scientists, clergymen, and other scholars. There are well-documented records about demons, readily available to those who do research in the subject. Throughout history concepts such as materializing and de-materializing, and manifestations in various physical forms, have been constant. These are frighteningly like what happens with UFOs and their occupants.

John Keel discusses this at some length, and comments that this is a major but little explored aspect of the UFO phenomenon—that it is theological and philosophical rather than purely scientific.[23] He goes on to say that the UFO problem can never be untangled by physicists and scientists unless they are men who also have been schooled in liberal arts, theology, and philosophy. As he rightly comments, most scientific disciplines are so demanding that their practitioners have little time or inclination to study other subjects which are somewhat outside their own immediate fields of interest.

Perhaps it is wise to add that it is dangerous deliberately to seek contact with UFO occupants—in the same sense that it is dangerous to become involved with black magic, for schizophrenia and even suicide can result, and at times have resulted, from such involvement.

Chapter 14

The Bible and UFOs

It is somewhat surprising to find how often ufologists refer to UFOs being associated with the Bible. At first sight this seems convincing, but closer examination reveals that much that is written is based on flimsy evidence. However, there are interesting conjectures, and not all should be dismissed out of hand. The subject would justify an in-depth study—even a further book—but for the moment we shall confine ourselves to a relatively brief survey.

Life on Other Planets?

Not everybody will accept the argument that UFOs and spiritism are in the same category. Therefore it is relevant to ask if the Bible allows the possibility of life on other planets: could that explain UFOs? The answer is that the Bible is silent on this subject. It is a revelation as to life on *this* planet, earth, and is not a textbook on biology, astronomy, or other sciences dealing with extraterrestrial life. While man has the right to believe that he is in unique relationship with God—with a special covenant for his salvation—he does not necessarily know that there are no other manlike creatures elsewhere in the creation of God.

Many—this author included—have some sort of deep-seated belief that there are no other "humans," but if it could be proved that there were other manlike beings, it would matter little. No Bible doctrine would thereby be put to one side.

Nevertheless the possibility of life on other planets, apart from divine creation, would be extremely unlikely. We discuss this in an appendix to *Crash Go the Chariots*. The late Dr. Frederick H. Giles, Jr., at that time Associate Professor of Physics and Astronomy at the University of South Carolina, cooperated to give the answers to a series of relevant questions. He outlined a number of difficulties to there even being a suitable planet with the right conditions for the maintenance of life. He pointed out that temperature was very important—if it was too high, the complexities of the chemical processes were such that they would not hold together. If the temperature was too low, the chemical processes would not occur rapidly enough for living things to arrive at a point of change, and therefore even the process of thinking would be out of the question. Such a planet would need to be commodious—it must not be too heavy or it would plaster life to its earth; it must not be too light, for some sort of atmosphere would need to be maintained. Then too the conjectured planet must be the right distance from the star it spun off, and also there would need to be a fantastically long period of time for the emergence of a self-replicating system.

Dr. Giles added that this applied merely to "life" itself, and that the emergence of sentient, conscious, intelligent life involved further problems. If all the other conditions were met, we would still need enough time for the complexity of intelligent life to appear. Even if there were intelligent beings, that would not necessarily mean that their technology would be highly developed. It would be an exceedingly complex operation for them to communicate with beings on earth or any other planet—even if they had the tremendous periods of time necessary for such an operation. At a conservative estimate it would take four light-years for a signal to be sent and received on earth, and then four more light-years for the return signal. By then the original operators would have been long since dead.

Dr. Giles further stated that Erich Von Daniken "has picked up some of the most conjectural areas of physics and astronomy and selected his own array of quite unconnected facts or suppositions, then built on them as though they were established and connected facts."

Asked to state again the basis for conjecture about other planets, Dr. Giles replied: "The only planet that we know for sure has life on it is the earth." He went on to say that some astronomers will calculate in terms of the probability of such bodies, but "they never use the terms of certainty which Von Daniken does."[1]

Neither Dr. Giles nor this author excluded the possibility of life on other planets, but certainly rejected the "there is no doubt" approach of Erich Von Daniken.

Life IS possible on other planets: if the Christian concept of creation is accepted, God the Creator could bring life into being according to His own will, wherever He chose. We have pointed to the problems associated with life on other planets, but the discussion does not end with "life." If the fact of UFOs from another planet is to be accepted, we must go beyond mere life. It must be highly intelligent life, with complex technological advancement, greatly superior to anything known on earth at least until very recent years.

This touches on another aspect of "UFOs and the Bible"—the subject of evolution and the possibility of spacemen having cohabited with women of the earth.

Ufologists Ask, "Are We Descended from Spacemen?"

First, to "tie the ends together," let it be said that if God is brought into the picture there is no problem as to life on other planets. Belief in an all-powerful God would mean there was no problem in believing He could create when and where He willed. In this volume we are not discussing the method of creation but the fact: that would involve more than a chance process without any control whatever. The mathematical possibilities against purely chance evolution are astronomical, and obviously they are further multiplied when the concept is extended to other planets. On purely academic grounds, a nontheistic theory of chance evolution is difficult to accept for the Christian. Many non-Christians tend either to take an agnostic attitude, leaving a mental question mark; or they take the view that they do not accept the concept of an Almighty God, and that to them "special creation" is inconceivable: therefore they leave themselves no alternative but to accept a chance evolutionary concept.

All this is relevant to much that is written by ufologists—not, however, in support of "special creation," but as supposed evidence that homo sapiens is descended from spacemen who visited the earth in ancient times. They point out that it is impossible to interbreed a man and an ape, and discuss the fact that man alone has a sense of destiny and a religious capacity. Typical writers along this line are Otto Binder and Max H. Flindt. They are not setting out to prove a biblical viewpoint as to man's creation, but are simply arguing that the riddle of man is resolved by seeing man's ancestors as coming from the stars.

Many ufologists believe that original man was created by a union of these beings from other planets with lower creatures on earth, and one argument commonly put forward by ufologists is that modern man could not have evolved on the earth without some outside assistance. Otto Binder submits a number of points to show that man could not merely be a product of evolution on the earth. He quotes liberally from Max H. Flindt, *On Tip-Toe Beyond Darwin,* and elaborates the hypothesis that possibly one or more of our ancestors came from outer space.

Binder submits that Flindt's argument is an answer to problems of evolution, claiming that the Darwinian-based hypothesis is unable to give satisfactory answers. We quote Binder as typical of the theories of a number of space writers at this point:[2]

As stated before, Darwin himself admitted at times that mankind in small ways fitted his evolution theory the least of all creatures. Alfred Wallace, his contemporary formulator of the theory of evolution, was even more emphatic, and forthrightly said that man was an exception to the orderly operation of biological laws, and that natural selection could not have operated in his case. What the true answer was he hazarded no guess.

Binder then quotes Flindt's theory as to man coming from a union between beings from the stars and earth creatures:[3]

And Flindt does give the answer that Wallace was unable to find, as a succinct question—"Is it because man's brain is an import?"
Namely, that man appeared so suddenly on the scene because he was a planned hybrid, a cross between superintelligent star men and subintelligent two-legged creatures on earth.

Later in his comments on this topic, Binder gives a list of the ways in which he claims man is unique and different from other creatures. He states that only man cries; that among the primates only man has bushy hair on top of his skull; that man has a supersensitive skin with a fine sense of touch which is denied to animals; that this last means that so much more information can be sent to a human brain because of stimuli to skin; that man swallows slowly, whereas with animals such as dogs food is virtually shot from the esophagus into the stomach; that man lacks tooth gaps; he does not have the penis bone that is associated with mammals and animals—a bone that rises within the penis before and during the sex act, whereas with human males emotion and blood supply are involved rather than a special bone. He goes on to discuss the very great differences relating to the brain and "imported mentality." He discusses the impossibility of interbreeding man with apes or other animals.

He refers to ancient men, many thousands of years before modern men, having a bigger brain capacity than modern man. This early "large brained subman" was one of our immediate ancestors, with a brain capacity three times that of a gorilla. His brain capacity is also three times that of other animals in proportion to their body weight, with a very much greater thinking capacity. He suggests that possibly this is the result of an interbreeding program with spacemen. He even makes the point that man alone possesses almost no bodily hair, whereas other creatures are hairy. He refers to the fact that the fertilized ovum of the human female is quite different from that of any other being, in that it buries itself in the woman's uterus wall.

Until writings such as these began to be prominent in recent times, most of the forthright opposition to the Darwin-based theory of evolution came from Christians who saw it as opposing the Bible. Now many ufologists reject Darwin on biological and other grounds. Many of their arguments were valid, but to insist that man has therefore resulted from a space–earth sexual union is conjectural. There is still no better explanation than that of Divine creation. We stress that we are not insisting on details as to special creation, including the method: that would be outside the scope of this volume. We are surveying only those biblical concepts which are relevant to the modern phenomena of UFOs and their occupants.

Giants on the Earth

A relevant topic, often referred to by ufogolists, is that of the giants of old. There are many legends about "semi-divine" beings, supposed to have resulted from sexual union between extraterrestrial beings and women of earth. In this connection Genesis 6: 5 in the Bible is quoted:

> There were giants in the earth in those days; and also after that, when the sons of God came in unto the daughters of men, and they bore children to them, the same became mighty, men which were of old, men of renown.

As with most controversial subjects, there are differing interpretations of this and the preceding verses. Bible scholars who take the verses literally are divided on what they mean. Some scholars suggest that "the sons of God" referred to were the godly line of Seth, while "the daughters of men" were from the ungodly line of Cain. Others believe that the so-called sons of God were fallen angels who then had sexual relations with women of earth, and giants were the result. Later on, the descendants of these people are called "Anakim"—giants—but in the Bible two different words for "giant" are associated with these people, one being the normal word for giants, in the sense we would use it today. This suggests they were normal humans, well above average in size. The grammatical construction in Genesis does not necessarily mean that giants resulted because of this union, in a cause-and-effect sense.

It is possible that the expression "There were giants in the earth in those days" is simply a statement of fact. Jesus said there is no marriage among the angels, and in that verse (Matthew 22: 30) He spoke of a future state where His followers would neither marry nor be given in marriage.

Those who hold to the argument that "the sons of God" were angelic beings point out that in the Book of Job (16:21; 38:7) and also in Daniel (3:25) such beings were angels, and there are other Scriptural references where the term is so used of angels. However, in other Scriptures (such as Psalm 73: 15) the godly among men are referred to as "the generation of thy sons"—the sons of God.

In their outstanding commentary on the Old Testament, Keil and Delitzsch point out that the term used at Genesis 6: 2 for "took them wives of all which they chose" includes a standard expression for "to take a wife" that is used throughout the whole of the Old Testament[4]—an expression referring to the marriage relationship that has been established by God at creation. These commentators go on to show that this never applied to the act of physical relationship as such. They then state, "This is quite sufficient of itself to exclude any reference to angels."

However, it is true that many scholars hold that these verses do refer to a union between angelic beings and women. If their view is correct, that could explain why there are so many legends around the world about gods having sexual relations with women, and godlike men being born to them. It is now recognized that legends usually have a basis in historical fact: this could be in that category.

Before we leave the subject, it is relevant to point out again that many supposed occupants of UFOs are not giants, but are in fact very small beings—often only four feet tall. Others are reported as monsters like apes, with others again having birdlike shapes and forms. These descriptions do not fit the idea of "giants in the earth."

UFOs in Israel's History?

Another supposed UFO in the Bible was the pillar of cloud and of fire at the time of the exodus of the Israelites from Egypt. Here was an aerial phenomenon, at times moving and at other times stationary, but always present with God's people.

A number of space writers tell us that this was a UFO. It was prominent at the parting of the Reed Sea (colloquially known as "the Red Sea") and the suggestion is that its "machinery" was vitally involved. Not only was there an "object" overhead (in the form of a cloud by day and a pillar of fire by night), but there was also the remarkable statement that the Israelites crossed this body of water "on dry ground" (Exodus 14: 22).

The Bible associates this with an especially strong east wind heaping up the waters, as shown at Exodus 14: 21. However, a normal wind would hardly dry up the mud, and a further extraordinary explanation is called for. Some ufologists suggest that an antigravitational beam was used by the "UFO," causing the waters to be forced back, and causing the ground itself to be "baked." As the Israelites were on the west side of the water, about to cross to the east side, the wind caused by the consequent air movement would be east (and west to the Egyptians on the opposite bank, meeting the blast going in the opposite direction).

If an antigravitational beam utilized electromagnetic forces, centering its action across the Sea of Reeds, heat could have been a side product of this beam. Thus the mud could have been completely dried out—virtually baked. The Israelites could, literally, have crossed on dry ground.

Another side effect would be that everything under the antigravitational beam would become, in layman's terms, very much heavier, for "weight" is linked to gravity. A film shown recently on Australian television suggested the possibility that when the Israelites actually crossed the Sea of Reeds, part of the beam was shielded, and that the shield was removed as the Egyptians crossed. This would help us to understand the statement at Exodus 14: 24 that "the Lord looked on the Egyptian army from the column of fire and cloud. . . . He took off their chariot wheels and made them move heavily."

If an antigravitational beam *was* employed, there would suddenly be great strain on the chariot axles, causing them to break. In this case, whether we believe in UFOs or not, "the Lord looked down" could well mean that He utilized an a-G beam. Bible miracles do not necessarily rule out laws of nature (including physics), but are often utilizations of those laws, especially involving synchronization so that at the right moment of time the "impossible" is accomplished. Belief in the omnipotent God makes possible also the belief in His power to so coordinate the forces of nature that His will must be accomplished at His word. If an antigravitational beam and an electromagnetic force were utilized, this merely means that the method would now be understood a little better.

Even if the visible cloud and fire were what we today would call a UFO—and this can only be conjectured, not proved—it would still not oppose Christian beliefs SO LONG as such an argument in no way limited Almighty God, in an absolute sense, to an airborne vehicle over the wilderness area through which the Hebrews traveled. Such a limitation would not be acceptable theologically, for the omnipresent God is not siimply a god of the plains or of the mountains or of the wilderness—a concept accepted by Israel's neighbors for their gods.

Nevertheless, the Israelites themselves were confined geographically, and for their sakes the presence of God *was* manifested in space and time. This was again shown in the Shekinah glory of the Temple, and at various other times, such as when the Lord spoke to Moses at the burning bush, and in the mountain where the Law was given.

Christian theology would certainly not limit the power of Almighty God to what could be accomplished from a UFO: on the other hand, if UFOs are a possibility, they could be utilized from time to time as a medium for the outworking of divine purposes.

Many space writers tend not to accept this reservation, and rather think of a god who *is* confined to a space vehicle. The difference is great, but there is a measure of agreement as to the possibility of the forces associated with UFO-type vehicles being utilized for God's purposes.

"Angels' Hair"

On that same wilderness journey to which we have referred, the people were supplied with a miraculous food, sometimes linked by ufologists to "angels' hair"—a very fine substance that has often been reported as dropping down from UFOs.

There are many reports of this "angels' hair"—one interesting case being in the January, 1970, issue of

Spacelink. Farmer Marius Magnan at Saint Ann, Manitoba, saw flying saucers over his property on September 18, 1968, and among other things he told of a substance floating down "just like popcorn popping from a corn popper." Samples were sent to scientific authorities and the material was examined by an infrared spectroscope. The substance was found to be of a cellulose nature, with fibers a uniform 1/200th millimeter in diameter. Further investigations showed that this so-called angels' hair was a rayon fiber coated with a gummy substance.

The biblical manna, that "food from heaven" that was so important to the Israelites for nearly forty years in the wilderness, is described in Exodus 16: 14, 15. We read that it was like coriander seed, white and tasting like wafers made with honey. The Israelites had to gather it early, for it melted with the heat of the sun (verse 21). "Angels' hair" also disintegrates very rapidly, usually when touched, but there the similarity seems to end. The manna could be kept without disintegrating, but after a day it would breed worms (verse 20), except for the supply gathered before the Sabbath (verse 24). The Sabbath's supply lasted for two days, not only one day, and this manna clearly is not the same substance as the nonlasting "angels' hair."

We have suggested the possibility of evil powers being associated with UFOs, and that same possibility is there with this substance. Some ufologists see a connection with the ectoplasm commonly associated with the séance room when materializations takes place.

To associate this "angels' hair" with manna is in the same category as associating Miriam's leprosy with the "burning sores" sometimes displayed by UFO contactees. Miriam (Moses' sister) was punished with temporary leprosy for taking a stand against Moses. Leprosy in the Old Testament does not necessarily mean leprosy as we think of it today, but was a more general term. After seven days Miriam was cured, so possibly hers was a relatively minor ailment. Some ufologists suggest it was a skin irritation caused by a UFO contact, but it would be as logical to suggest she was bitten by a scorpion or a lizard. There simply is no evidence as to what the "leprosy" was, apart from it being a punishment inflicted by God, with visible consequences.

As we have said, to associate her "leprosy" with a UFO has about as much factual basis as the association of manna with "angels' hair." One or two points of similarity certainly do not justify an enthusiastic complete identification.

The Pillar of Cloud . . . and Crossing the Jordan

The same would apply to the supposed presence of a UFO at the burning bush when the Lord spoke to Moses—for this claim is also made by space writers. It is stretching the record in Exodus, chapter 3, to suggest that the nonconsumed burning bush was in fact a UFO.

It is relevant, then, to ask further, "Could the 'pillar of cloud by day' and the 'pillar of fire by night' possibly have been a UFO?" It certainly was a moving aerial object, and God Himself was associated with it (Exodus 13: 21, 22; 14: 19, etc.). If evil forces can use UFOs, as we suggest in our chapter on paraphysical manifestations, certainly such vehicles could be available for the purposes of Almighty God.

However, the record shows that this "something" was permanently visible, by both day and night—constantly and continuously. UFOs are at best a poor imitation, visible, relatively speaking, for only short periods of time. If our earlier analysis is correct, they are necessarily so limited. They are usually seen for very short periods, then they swiftly disappear. Longer visits often—not always—involve hypnosis, and doubt sometimes lingers as to the actuality of the experience outside the contactee's own mind.

Once again, there is a very great contrast between UFOs, the pillar of cloud, and the pillar of fire. The pillar was always visible, at any time of the day or the night—not just for a few seconds, or even for a few hours. Even the sighting in New Guinea by Reverend

Gill and so many reputable witnesses was only for a few hours, and not day after day, and night after night, and month after month, as in the wilderness experience.

The same explanation as for the Red (Reed) Sea could also apply to the crossing of the Jordan. Archaeologically, an interesting possibility is that this blocking of the Jordan from Adam (now Damieh) to Jericho could be associated with a landslide at Damieh, about eighteen miles north of Jericho. At least twice in recorded history (1267 and 1927) the Jordan has been completely blocked following a landslide, for sixteen hours and twenty-one hours, respectively. This is a reasonably satisfactory "natural" explanation, with a remarkable synchronization of events as Joshua and his men took their step of faith.

However, if the Bible account is to be taken literally, that explanation is only partially acceptable. The record clearly states that the middle of the Jordan River was immediately dry, and that all Israel crossed over on dry ground (Joshua 3: 17). While it can be argued that the method of the miracle is not revealed, it is possible that the same principles were utilized as were suggested for the Red Sea miracle. Some would say it does not matter; others would say it is even wrong to look for the "natural" explanation to a miracle; on the other hand, some who have never accepted the landslide explanation might find the antigravitational beam concept more acceptable. We are not dogmatic on the answer, but merely suggest the possibilities, partly because the incident is tied in to UFOs by some space writers.

Elijah Taken to Heaven

A measure of similarity to a UFO "happening" can be argued for the ascension of Elijah in a chariot of fire (2 Kings 2: 11). Whatever happened, it seems that the younger prophet Elisha saw the phenomenon as a chariot of fire and a chariot of horses. Again there are opposite interpretations as to what this could mean. On the one hand, Hebrew writing often combined the symbolic and the literal in a way that is not typical of Western literature—it was not always possible to separate them. Thus "Egypt" could mean the land, or could be a synonym for "captivity," and similarly the description of chariots of fire and of horses could simply be a descriptive way of saying that Elijah was taken in full view of Elisha.

This view is possibly strengthened by the association of the term "whirlwind" or "tempestuous storm," used at verses 1 and 11. Keil and Delitzsch state that this "was frequently the herald of the divine self-revelations in the terrestrial world (vid. Job 38: 1; 40: 6; Ezek. 1: 4; Zech. 9: 14)".[5] This type of language is therefore seen as the method whereby human language and experience are used to explain what otherwise would be unexplainable. On this interpretation it would be quite unnecessary to insist that the chariots were actually UFOs. To quote Keil and Delitzsch again (though they are not referring to UFOs):[6]

> All further questions, e.g., concerning the nature of the fiery chariot, the place to which Elijah was carried, the day of his ascension ... are to be set down as useless trifles.

If it be insisted that the biblical description is entirely literal, then it would seem that a UFO, according to modern concepts, should be ruled out. There is no modern description of a UFO looking like a chariot of horses. As with "angels' hair" and Miriam's leprosy, it is stretching the facts to see a complete identification with a UFO. All that modern sightings have done, so far as this incident is concerned, is to indicate that Elijah's ascension is not impossible after all. Once again, if the method of that ascension bears similarities to the workings of a UFO, there is no real problem. Bible miracles often utilize natural laws: if UFOs also operate by those laws, there could at times be similarities in visible outworkings. The similarity might well be restricted to

the utilization of the laws independently of an actual
vehicle such as a UFO.

The Vision of Ezekiel

What about Ezekiel's "spacecraft"—a UFO? This is
seized on by space writers, as though it was the most
convincing of all the biblical evidence about UFOs. In
fact it is not. It was somewhat of a surprise to find that
Dr. Barry H. Downing, in *The Bible and Flying Saucers*, tends to "low-key" this incident so far as association with flying saucers is concerned. He points out that
Ezekiel alone seems to have had this vision.[7]

Ezekiel himself puts the whole incident and its ac-
companying prophecies in the realm of vision—"I saw
visions of God" (1: 1). His descriptions are in the form
of symbol and allegory, more so than with most other
biblical prophets. He elaborates the most minute details, not only in the vision of the wheels in chapter 1,
but at many other places throughout his prophecy.
Chapters 16 and 22 are good examples of that same al-
legorical style where space writers would not suggest
"UFO influence."

From Ezekiel's vision of the wheels we learn much
about the Being of God—for Ezekiel's vision is of a
theophany, an appearance or manifestation of God.
Theologians of various schools have great difficulty in
interpreting the vision of the wheels and of the glory of
God. It appears to ennoble and spiritualize some concepts known in the surrounding Babylonian culture,
such as the beings described as part-animal and part-
man in appearance. It describes the Being of God
whose "movements" are in all directions at the one
time; it also describes His messengers who are swift to
do His will.

Erich Von Daniken writes at length about this
"space vehicle" and claims that the gods "took him
with them in their vehicle."[8] Von Daniken does not accept that Ezekiel was here in touch with an Almighty
God, for in that same context he states that "this kind

of locomotion seems to me to be quite incompatible with the idea of an Almighty God."

It is stretching the record to say that Ezekiel was taken in a space vehicle, for, as we have already seen, Ezekiel himself attributes the revelations to divine vision, not to physical transportation. The vision was apparently not even seen by his fellow captives by the River Chebah (Ezekiel 1: 1).

Nevertheless Erich Von Daniken makes a relevant point when he suggests that such locomotion is incompatible with the idea of an Almighty God. God does not need a space vehicle, a UFO to move around in. He is omnipresent and omnipotent—everywhere present and all-powerful. He does not need a UFO, teleportation, or the utilization of antigravitational and/or electromagnetic forces. He speaks and it is done. He whispers and the hills re-echo. His servants might well utilize the principles by which UFOs can operate, for God is the very Creator of those principles and laws.

Those laws originate with Him, but it is also possible that at present they can be misused, even as is shown in the New Testament where evil forces make use of "powers and signs and lying wonders" (2 Thess. 2: 9). That passage goes on to say that deception and delusion will be involved with those lying wonders when men will not believe the truth.

UFOs in the New Testament?

We have glanced at the possibility of UFOs in the Old Testament. What about the New Testament? One incident often linked to a UFO by ufologists, and included in a recent Australian television presentation, is the "Star of Bethlehem," mentioned at Matthew, chapter 2. In this connection UFO writers at times refer to apocryphal books which are not included in the accepted canon of the Christian Bible. They mention "The Tale About the Three Magi," and suggest this indicates that Jesus descended from a star.

It is true there is such a writing, but the vehicle was also described as having wings like an eagle's wings, and the earliest possible date for its writing is the middle of the third century A.D. There are various writings about it through the centuries. However, to quote such a writing—acknowledged as written some 200 years after the event—is hardly acceptable as evidence that the "Star of Bethlehem" was a flying saucer which directed the wise men toward the place where the Babe was then living.

These "wise men from the east" came to Jerusalem to find the Christ Child, born King of the Jews (verse 2). They were granted an audience with King Herod, who first ascertained from the chief priests and scribes that the Old Testament Scriptures pinpointed Bethlehem as the place where the Christ would be born. Herod sent the wise men off to Bethlehem, and we read that once again they saw the star—it went before them and then remained stationary over where the Child was.

Whatever the answer is, it is by no means sure that these wise men followed the star all the way from their "eastern" country. Babylonians were famous for astrology in ancient times, and the tradition still persisted at the time of Christ. Their knowledge of "the star of the King of the Jews" might not have come only from their study of heavenly bodies, but also from the Jews themselves. At the time of the return of the Jews from the Babylonian exile in 537 B.C. a great colony of Jews remained. They had some of the Old Testament Scriptures, as did the priests who did "research" at the direction of Herod in Jerusalem. It would seem the wise men had not been given this specific information as to Bethlehem, for they came to Jerusalem, not Bethlehem. Jerusalem was by now the capital city, and it would be a reasonable assumption to inquire for the king at the nation's capital.

Possibly they did not see the "star" all the time, for if so, they would probably have kept on going, farther south to Bethlehem. Another possible clue is that when

Herod sent them off to Bethlehem, there is an exclamation, "and, lo, the star, which they saw in the east, went before them. . . ." It almost seems as if they now saw it again after a lapse of time. That does not rule out the physical reality of the star, though it does suggest that possibly this was not their "personal UFO," leading them every separate mile of their very long journey. Opinions vary on this.

Was it a UFO as so many ufologists claim? The record implies that it was some sort of special sign in the sky, and that it could move from the east and then remain motionless over where the Christ Child was now living. However, there the similarity to UFOs appears to end, for as we search the record in Matthew relating to the birth of Christ, five times we are told of divine messages being given—not from a spacecraft, but in a dream (Mat. 1: 20; 2: 12, 13, 19, 22). There are other occasions when we read of God's will being revealed in a dream, and there is no reason to doubt that the communication *was* given in that way. If it had actually been from a spacecraft, the record would surely have been clear: the Hebrews could accept a constantly visible pillar of cloud from which God would at times speak, and chariots of fire and of horses with Elijah, and a heavenly vision of "wheels" with Ezekiel. The concept of beings stepping out of a spacecraft would not have been difficult for these men of the Bible, but the record is clear: the revelation was by dream, on five separate occasions, to the wise men and to Joseph and Mary alike.

A Principle Divinely Utilized?

Possibly the star was a divine utilization of the principles by which UFOs operate, as a special sign that was so very appropriate for those men of the East with their traditions of astronomy and astrology. There is certainly no indication that it was a UFO manned by "spacemen." On that conjecture the Bible is simply silent. The earlier incident of the angelic chorus over the "shepherds' fields" was not associated with this "Star," being months—possibly as long as two years— earlier. The wise men brought their gifts to a house, not to the stable or the inn where Jesus had been born—on this commentators are agreed.

This chapter on UFOs and the Bible is just that—a chapter, not a detailed analysis. Therefore let it merely be stated briefly that many other New Testament incidents are identified by ufologists as linked with UFOs, but cannot be supported as such. The baptism of Jesus, His temptation in the wilderness, His ascension, the conversion of Saul of Tarsus on the road to Damascus—these are all put forward by ufologists as involving UFOs, though sometimes one finds it hard to follow the logic of the argument. This is true even with serious writers such as Dr. Barry H. Downing:[9]

> It seems consistent to argue that if Jesus "ascended" in some sort of UFO, the same vehicle brought him to Paul's company on the Damascus Road.

Perhaps "it seems consistent" but it certainly is not convincing. Jesus is the Son of God and He does not need a UFO. After He had risen from the dead He was no longer restricted by laws to which He had previously been voluntarily subject. Now He would walk about eight miles to Emmaus, despite dreadful crucifixion wounds and He could even walk through a closed door; He would assure His disciples that He would be with them always—surely this did not mean in tens of thousands of UFOs, all at the same moment of time— across the many cultures of the world?

The New Testament teaches that Jesus "emptied Himself" (Philippians 2: 7, 8), even to the point of death on a cross. The same passage claims resurrection life for Jesus, a new life that in a number of ways was different from His life before His crucifixion. It seems He was now independent of the laws of nature by which He had allowed Himself to be restricted.

This author believes that "independence" is much

nearer the truth in the ascension of Jesus than the suggestion put forward by some writers that He ascended in a UFO. The claim is that the statement, "a cloud received Him out of their sight" (Acts 1: 9), means that the "cloud" was in fact a UFO, and that the "cloud" so often associated with divine manifestations and revelations was that same UFO. It is conjecture, quite unprovable, and again it is in the category of incidents already referred to—points of similarity are there but complete identification is going beyond the facts given in the record.

Limiting Jesus to the use of UFOs is to restrict His deity and His power as the Son of God Who rose from the dead and resumed the divine attribute of spiritual omnipresence.

Similarly, to insist that the second coming of Christ will involve huge "fleets" of UFOs is no more than interesting conjecture, very possibly over-literalizing some of the descriptive passages in the Apocalypse (the Revelation) beyond what was ever intended. Possibly physical laws involved with UFOs could also be utilized in that second coming, but without the need for "material" or "solid" vehicles as such.

UFOs and Armageddon

That leads to our last subject—the fact of the continuing battle of the forces of evil against the holy and Almighty God. This book is not a theological textbook, and so we do not elaborate the theology but rather accept the fact of that conflict as it is given in the Bible. There we learn that a final "Battle of Armageddon" will take place when the forces of evil will be destroyed.

This association of Armageddon with UFOs is taken very seriously by some Bible students. There are various "schools" when it comes to Bible prophecies, and one of those schools is the so-called futurist school which believes that the return of Jesus Christ is to be in this generation. Part of the belief stems from the statement of Jesus, "This generation shall not pass till all these things be fulfilled." In the same context, He spoke of the fig tree putting forth its leaves, this being a sign that summer was nigh. Jesus then went on to say that in the same way, when the signs which He referred to became apparent, His disciples should look up, for their redemption was drawing nigh. Luke, chapter 21, is a relevant passage.

The fig tree is a symbol of Israel as a nation, and it is interesting to realize that the fig tree was indeed putting forth its leaves in 1947, and Israel's modern nationhood was declared in 1948. The modern rash of UFO sightings is usually taken to start from 1947, and if there is some fantastic plan being developed, its outworking would seem to coincide with the generation to which Jesus pointed—if the interpretation according to the futurist school of prophecy is correct.

We have already suggested what a dreadful thing it would be if there are thousands upon thousands of people across the face of the globe, conditioned by hypnotic suggestion, ready at a given signal to obey, no matter what the consequences, and not even knowing beforehand that they are ready to obey. Obviously, terrible chaos could be created.

The Lord Jesus warned that at the end of the age there would be great signs in the heavens, and it could well be that the UFO phenomenon of this generation should be included in that category. We also saw that the New Testament associates the activities of Satan with power and signs and lying wonders. Undoubtedly much that we read of with UFO activities would fit into those categories.

Even if this prophetic view is not all the answer to UFOs, one can only conclude that the mission of the UFO occupants is impossible. Sightings have taken place now for thousands of years, and, whatever the reason, earth has not been invaded by hostile beings from outer space. The super-plans are apparently offset by an even greater plan, determined by God Himself.

A Takeover Attempt?

Is there to be an attempt at a takeover? There surely are limitations to the life-giving powers of these UFO creatures, and that itself would imply that their mission is impossible. Man is the master of the animals, and despite seemingly way-out theories, such as monster insects waiting to attack us, in fact man is still able to control the lesser creatures. If through the long centuries of apparently serious sightings, animals have been part of the sinister plans of hostile beings, again it must be concluded that their mission is impossible. Animals have not been transformed, taken over by beings whose minds are totally opposed to man's welfare, and now having access to bodies stronger than those of men. If some such plan were seriously thought of, again we would conclude that the mission is impossible: it has failed.

There is no evidence that these people have produced a race superior to man. If it is true that they are using men, women, boys, and girls to serve their own purposes, the usefulness of those who thereby become their servants is limited to one generation. They are unable even to double the life span, let alone give men the fantastic life spans that would be necessary to move through the planetary systems of the galaxies that are beyond our present knowledge. It would appear that these people need a super race, unfettered by the fear of death, to accomplish their purposes. To find such a race on this earth is a "Mission Impossible."

Is it a spiritual takeover that is intended? Unless we conclude that success is measured by the widespread evidence of witchcraft and spiritism, we can only conclude that, despite all the appearances and contacts through the centuries, mankind has not been subdued by these creatures.

Our chapter has been dealing with UFOs and the Bible. Many other aspects and incidents could be referred to, and are mentioned in various books and journals.

The destruction of the cities of Sodom and Gomorrah—discussed at length in this author's *Crash Go the Chariots*—is one such, but on examination the evidence for UFO activity is flimsy. Scientists associated with the Dead Sea Chemical Industry Co. issued a paper reconstructing what they thought had happened: the destruction was probably linked with the igniting of an oil basin beneath the southern part of the Dead Sea. Evidence that the earth's layers were ruptured—including the top level of rock salt—is convincing, including great quantities of those layers, united as by fire, at the top of nearby Jebel Usdum (the Arabic name for Mount Sodom).

Other space writers major on the more benevolent acts, and the many references to angels in the Bible. The inference is that they move around our planet by means of UFOs. There is no entirely convincing evidence for this theory, but even if there were, it would simply mean that the method was thereby better understood. Belief in angels, and in the great Creator-God, would mean belief also in His power to make possible the accomplishment of His will throughout the universe.

However, as we have already said, it seems more likely that certain principles are utilized, rather than UFOs as such. Angelic beings would hardly be limited by laws of gravity—they are spiritual beings, not "contained" by flesh and blood. Nor do they all need wings, as artists have so often suggested. Creatures of earth are limited by time and space, but that does not apply to heavenly beings. Nor do angels in the will and service of God need to convince men by displays of material or physical strength.

To argue that God's heavenly messengers need UFOs to achieve His purposes is to limit God's powers, and His thoughts, to those of men. Much of the modern writing about UFOs and the Bible tends to think of God as little more than a glorified astronaut. The Bible shows Him as omnipresent, omnipotent, and omniscient, and His heavenly servants are not limited by earth's laws of physics. The physical principles by which UFOs operate might well be utilized for the purposes of God, but the Bible certainly does not confine Almighty God to a heavenly "super-car."

Chapter 15

Conclusion: A Personal Note

Throughout this volume we have looked at a number of possible explanations for the UFO phenomenon. Many who have no interest in spiritual concepts will immediately reject out of hand the possible association with evil powers. I have found that many people are prepared to discuss other possibilities in a way that was unacceptable ten or fifteen years ago, but today they are more "respectable" because it has been increasingly recognized that there really is a UFO phenomenon. However, when it is suggested that the answer is possibly of a spiritual nature, very often there is a mental switching-off. Other possibilities can be rationally discussed, and can be investigated with an unbiased mind. It is as though there is a prejudged acceptance of the fact that the answer cannot possibly be in any way "spiritual." I suggest this is illogical—and unfair to those who hold such a point of view.

A number of people have written to me about my earlier book, *Crash Go the Chariots*, expressing surprise that somebody who can write M.A., B.D., Ph.D., after his name can believe in a God, and even in demons. My own conviction is that many of those people are unaware of the total picture, and usually are products of a rather narrow culture, affluent with at materialism that does not need to admit the possibility of spiritual realities. Move those people away from Australia, USA, England, and other countries with Christian influences (even if it is not practiced to the extent it should be), and put them into certain other countries where Christianity is not widely accepted, and their attitude to spiritual realities—even to evil forces—would be radically changed.

Evil Forces Are Real

I have lived in such countries, and have moved around them extensively. Even apart from my strong Christian beliefs, and my acceptance of the Bible as the revealed Word of God, I would have no doubt whatever as to the fact of spiritual beings, evil forces, and phenomena that cannot be explained by purely physical, psychical, or psychological concepts.

All that is background to what many will say is a "way-out" suggestion as to the mission of these UFOs. We have suggested the possibility of brainwashing of contactees, and even of hypnotic influences. We suggested that thereby activities would be undertaken at a given signal, a signal of which the contactee at present has no knowledge whatever. We have also suggested that sometimes the "messages" given are accurate— such as the predictions of the assassination of Robert Kennedy and of Martin Luther King—but that predictions relating to the end of the world have been shown to be inaccurate, and unfulfilled.

Why do these UFO messages so often refer to the end of the world? Why is Armageddon specifically mentioned? These beings have amazing knowledge of individuals and could well be versed in teachings about biblical prophecies. The Bible says the rebel spiritual forces "believe and tremble." Are they determined to make a last-ditch stand, in a desperate bid to foil that prophecy as to their own ultimate destruction? It sounds fantastic—but so does much associated with UFOs.

If there is truth in this hypothesis, preparations would be going on—just in case those overheard futurist interpretations happened to be correct. Indeed, much of this interpretation would apply to other prophetic teachings as well, at least as to the basic teaching of a final and conclusive battle between the spiritual forces of good and evil.

In this argument we are developing, it is relevant that Jesus said that no man knows the day or the hour of His return—that this knowledge is restricted to God.

In the Bible, the return of Christ and the Battle of Armageddon are separated, and we are not confusing the two. However, they are related—Armageddon cannot eventuate until after Christ's return. When the first is eventually fulfilled, the latter will be relatively near at hand.

Part of the remarkable genius of the Christian message is that, as the generations have come and gone, there has been a continuing hope that Christ would establish His Kingdom during the generation of the church then living. Then, in relatively recent years, there has been greatly increased emphasis on the possibility of that return in this very generation. We have seen that occupants of these UFOs know all sorts of details about people, even concerning their thinking patterns. What if they know in great detail the teaching of the futurist school of prophetic interpretation?

When Does "This Generation" Start?

Many of that school believe that "this generation" to which Jesus referred started on May 14, 1948, when the modern state of Israel was proclaimed. They are not always agreed as to the length of a generation—for the Hebrew it could have been twenty-five or forty years, or even seventy years if it be a full lifetime, but the basic argument remains unaltered. Even if other details propounded by the "futurist school" are rejected, the basic hypothesis of recruitment because of that coming Armageddon could still be relevant.

Kenneth Arnold's sighting in 1947 is accepted by most ufologists as the starting point for the tremendously increased number of sightings—literally tens of thousands and more—that have taken place in this generation. Even before that sighting, "futurists" were making much of the fact that very many thousands of Jews had returned to Palestine (now Israel), just as, centuries before, the Bible had declared would happen. No other people have been scattered to the four winds and then brought back into their land as these people have been brought back. All around the world many preachers have been proclaiming this as a direct fulfillment of prophecy. Parallel with that seeming fulfillment was the further prediction that the return of Christ was soon to take place. Had not He Himself said that when the fig tree (a symbol of Israel's nationhood) put forth its leaves, with signs in the heavens, men should look up because their redemption drew nigh? There certainly are signs in the heavens today—thousands of them, in the many-shaped UFOs sighted all around the world.

If all this proclamation of prophetic truth is known to those paraphysical entities reported as the occupants of UFOs, could not this greatly increased UFO activity stem from their age-long fear that soon they face the dread Battle of Armageddon? The Bible has pointed to that through the centuries.

Armageddon—Mount Megiddo ("Har" is the Hebrew word for "Mount")—is a literal place. We have seen that spiritual realities are at times described in symbolic terms in the Bible, even utilizing actual place names, but it is also possible that in this instance there is a literal concept of a great battle at a particular place—Mount Megiddo. It even seems that physical aspects and powers will be combined with spiritual counterparts. The Bible suggests that spiritual powers as well as mankind will be involved in that great conflict between the forces of good and of evil. Mankind will be involved—and the Satanic forces will need all the mankind that can be pressed into service.

We have also stressed the possibility that a great pattern of brainwashing is taking place. Are men and women being influenced, even "possessed," so that when the signal is given they will be ready to give total allegiance to these beings who will then show themselves as their masters? Is this why there is such greatly increased activity in UFOs, and Ouija boards, Satan worship, séances, and all sorts of dabblings that even a generation ago were regarded as foolish and evil? Today there is a great increase in these things, and even in this decade there has begun an accelerating swing away from drugs as the "in" thing, to Satan worship and séances as the new "in" thing. Is a great army being recruited by beings who know that, if they are unsuccessful in this last great conflict, their doom is dreadful indeed?

If this theory is correct, some will ask, "Why did they bother to influence so many who have already died?" The answer could be that they do not know the hour of battle, and they must be active whenever it is possible to be active. Jesus clearly said that God alone knows the time of the last great happenings. Thus they will enroll all they can in case *this* is the year, or the month, or even the day.

Beings with Limited Power

However, in various ways we have seen that their powers are limited. It is as though God Himself has said, "Thus far shall you go and no further." There was once a famous Jewish teacher who warned his own colleagues and leaders not to fight against the Christian teaching that Jesus had risen from the dead. "If this teaching is of man, it will come to nothing," he told them. "However, if it be of God, you cannot overthrow it—you might find yourselves fighting against God" (Acts 5: 38, 39). There is a parallel with these UFO occupants who are opposed to that same Almighty God.

To many, the hypothesis we have just outlined will be totally unacceptable, fantastic, one to which minds are immediately closed. However, a wise man might well ponder it, and consider many facts which would seem to make this theory at least worthy of consideration. If it is truth, then those same Bible prophecies which have had an amazing habit of being fulfilled in the past will prove to be true once again.

One last point should be touched on. Many who have read this book will wonder if they should fear the power of the devil. To the person who is a true Christian the answer is "No." "If God is for us, who can be against us? . . . Who shall separate us from the love of God? . . . I am persuaded that . . . neither principalities nor powers . . . can separate us from the love of God which is in Christ Jesus our Lord" (Romans 8: 31, 35, 38, 39).

The Christian's superior position is beautifully illustrated by an incident with the prophet Elisha. A young man with him was very fearful because of the great enemy host surrounding the city of Dothan—those forces had come out especially to capture Elisha.

"Fear not," said Elisha to the young man. "Those who are with us are more than those with them" (2 Kings 2: 16).

How could that be? The city was surrounded—horses and chariots and a great host.

"Open his eyes, Lord, that he may see," Elisha prayed. It seems that Elisha already "saw"—certainly he already believed! "And the Lord opened the eyes of the young man, and he saw: and behold, the mountain was full of horses and chariots of fire round about Elisha" (verse 17).

"Those with us" are still more than "those with them." No disciple of Jesus Christ need be obsessed with fear because of opposing spiritual powers, whether manifested in UFOs or in other nonterrestrial form.

The forces of evil will be routed, and the purposes of the Eternal and Holy God will stand. Evil principalities, wicked spiritual beings with much power in this age of testing, will eventually be overthrown. When they set themselves against Almighty God theirs must ultimately prove to be a "Mission Impossible."

Chapter 16

An Update:
The Alien Agenda Progresses

In an earlier chapter we quoted Professor Allen Hynek as stating, "The part we ignore may contain the clue to the whole subject." We went on to ask, "Is that clue in the realm of spirits and demons?"

Have I Changed My Mind?

As I lecture in countries as far removed as the United States and Australia, I am asked questions such as, "Have you changed your mind?" Sometimes scholars have even asked me if I'm serious and if I'm embarassed to talk about UFOs and demonic forces in the same breath?

My answer is unequivocal. Not only have I not changed my mind but I have become even more convinced as to the rightness of the hypothesis put forward in these pages.

Let me tell you a strange story. I shall change the name of the person concerned for very good reasons. The story is absolutely factual and I have photocopied documents in my possession covering the material I now present.

The Start of a Bizarre Experience

I was lecturing in a Christian college in California. It was a summer course, involving several lectures a day. During a break a message came to me—"Dr. Wilson, there is a long distance call for you." I answered the call, and it was the start of one of the most bizarre experiences of my life.

"I'm Murray Cooper. You've probably not heard of me, but I've had a series of experiences with UFOs and I'm scared out of my wits. Can you help me?"

He had read my book *UFOs and Their Mission Impossible* and thought that maybe there was some way I could help him. "What do you mean, 'experiences with UFOs?' " I asked.

"Can you ring me back?" he asked. "I'm not on my own telephone." He gave me a number, and having been given permission from the professor in whose office I was sitting, I did call him back. Perhaps I should see what I could do.

Whether that was a good decision or not is debatable. What started with a single call became many over a period of weeks. To this day I don't know all the answers to the facts and fantasies I was given.

This man had indeed had "UFO experiences," including disappearances from home, missing time for which he could not account, physical marks on his body, and—perhaps strangest of all—an incredible increase in knowledge in areas where previously he had been quite uninformed. On one occasion he tried (on the telephone) to tell me of his spiritual searchings, but his voice slowed down, deepened, and then gurgled into nothingness. The phone went dead.

I called him back, but there was no immediate answer. I tried again several times, and eventually got back to him. He believed—probably rightly—that "they" did not want him to talk to me about spiritual things. Dire consequences would follow—to him and me.

The contact continued over a period, but a change had taken place. No longer was he grasping, searching, desperately needing help. Now he was the Messiah, the one specially chosen by the gods from outer space to bring the true message of peace for all men from their brethren beyond the stars. He had a key role in the Agenda of the Aliens.

He would send me proof. And in due course material arrived as promised. One of the first evidences that

218

he was a "prophet" who must be taken seriously was
that he had foretold where a meteorite would land in
California, with his predictions properly dated, quite
conclusively. Then came the later newspaper reports—
his predictions had come true.

Vastly Increased Knowledge

Then there was a map of the heavens—planets, and
constellations, and so much more. This was from a
college drop-out who had not previously demonstrated
a special interest let alone a specialized knowledge of
such matters.

It was even more eerie to receive his handwritten
extracts of New Testament writings—in perfect New
Testament Greek. Most disturbing yet was a written
message warning Wilson to keep off.

Easily explained? He'd simply copied the N.T.
Greek? Had he traced a map of the heavens? Had he
faked the gurgling, deep voice and was an egotistical
impressionist seeking attention and publicity? Had he
added the note of warning to me for publicity's sake because I was becoming known as a writer in the area of
UFOs, gods from outer space, and various forms of
psychic phenomena? Maybe. But read on.

A Radio Hook-Up With Dr. Hynek

I was sitting in my home in Melbourne, Australia.
The telephone rang and soon I found myself quite un-
expectedly on an international telephone hook-up, in a
radio presentation dealing with UFOs.

There had been a mysterious disappearance over the
Tasman Sea, between Melbourne and Tasmania. There
was serious conjecture that a pilot and his plane had
been "hijacked" by strange beings from outer space.
Did I believe this to be a convincing UFO experience,
or just another hoax? Or had the pilot simply become

disoriented as some of the mocking scoffers were insisting?

I was somewhat surprised at being involved, especially when I found that the expert from the U.S.A. (also on the international hook-up) was none other than Professor J. Allen Hynek.

I did not know how this most recent incident was to be explained. It might well be something to do with human error, machine failure, or some other quite commonplace happening, even if we did not at this point know what it was.

Dr. Hynek was also unsure, and he certainly did not commit himself to a UFO abduction as the explanation. However, he also very soberly cautioned against all UFOs being written off as just "twinkling stars." This was one of the world's leading astronomers talking. He was not some "crackpot" who shouted "UFO!" every time a satellite was seen in the starry sky, or when one of the glorious heavenly phenomena was especially impressive.

No. This was the man whose special and official role was to debunk all UFO sightings, as made clear in "Project Blue Book." His change of heart had come slowly, but it had been forced on him. He could find an explanation for most of the sightings and experiences he investigated, but there was a small percentage that could *not* be explained—except by the paraphysical explanation which we present in this book.

As I shared in that radio hook-up I felt that I had a good deal of common ground with this highly respected man of science.

A Talk With Dr. Hynek

Months went by. I was again in the United States, and knew that in a couple of weeks I would be in Chicago. I called Dr. Hynek's office at the University of Illinois at Urbana, outside Chicago. "I'm Dr. Clifford Wilson," I told his secretary. "I'll be passing through

Chicago. Perhaps I could meet up with Dr. Hynek?"

The response was warm, and in due time I was in his office. He had some of my writings there—apparently not just because I was visiting! We talked at length, and obviously had areas of very real agreement. He told me something of his personal "journey," along the lines of what was already in his well-known *The UFO Experience: A Scientific Inquiry*.

He had come to believe that with a small percentage of UFO experiences their paraphysical nature must be recognized. He believed in living forces that were not of this earth, but not from other planets as such either. To him these beings were not necessarily evil (as they were, and are, to this writer). Certainly they must be taken seriously, for their reality had been clearly demonstrated. Of that he was convinced.

Back to Murray Cooper

Now let us return briefly to Murray Cooper (remembering that is not his name, but otherwise this record is totally factual). We told how Murray Cooper had drawn maps and diagrams of heavenly bodies—Dr. Hynek's area of expertise. But not only did right-handed Murray draw those maps of previously unknown phenomena. He drew them left-handed.

And that is not all. Dr. Hynek and other University researchers conducted their own investigations. (I have a photocopied list of professional people so involved as witnesses). They went to Murray's home, and they watched him in a trance-like state, drawing, writing, listing and enumerating data. They saw his hand, his left hand, moving. But there was no paper in front of him—as they watched, the writing appeared on a scratch pad in another room.

They watched him drawing the UFO in which he had been "abducted." They saw the marks of some of the etchings on the Nazca Plains copied on to his body. They heard his wife testify to the strange experiences her husband had endured, of non-human beings who had terrorized her and of her decision to leave him. This highly intelligent being who was obsessed with higher physics and "new" astronomy was not the very ordinary, considerate person she had married. He had become, literally, a man possessed.

"What is your explanation?" I asked Dr. Hynek. He had no clear answer. By now we shared much common ground relating to Murray Cooper. Five years before this he would have regarded such "experiences" as rubbish. Had he not debunked story after story, descrediting the witnesses, ridiculing their testimony, refusing to give an inch to such nonsense?

Little green men! Visits to unmapped planets! Contacts from outer space! Crackpots who talked such absurdities should be exposed. And expose them he had, very effectively. Until in honesty he was forced to admit there was something. He had no conviction whatever that people had visited other planets, but he did become convinced that they believed they had had such experiences. To them the experience was real—even though it was somehow implanted into their minds by powerful, non-human, living forces.

Murray Cooper was one such contact. His experiences were real to him. He had not really visited the places he talked and wrote about, but his mind had been taken over. Knowledge and belief of such experiences had been impressed into his memory bank.

Dr. Hynek's investigation had proved to be baffling but convincing. The man he watched was demonstrating automatic writing, was displaying knowledge beyond what he could have been taught in any university, and was utterly sincere in his detailed descriptions of the UFO, its occupants, and his own experiences with them.

Professor Hynek did not wish to identify those entities as "human" or as "evil," for that would be going across a border which at that time was closed to him. He did not want to be linked with demons, but he did clearly acknowledge "another dimension," a force beyond human explanation.

A False Messiah

All we have written about Murray Cooper *can* be explained. Jesus said that at the end times there would be false prophets and false evidences as signs in the heavens. The UFO phenomenon and Murray Cooper's experiences fit the category. In fact, we go further. Jesus also said there would be false messiahs.

Murray Cooper not only believes he is the Messiah, especially chosen by the space gods to offer peace to the world. He has produced a meandering statement (by automatic writing) in which he offers himself and the forces he represents as the world's only hope.

Jesus said, "false messiahs." And there have already been a number of these self-proclaimed "messiahs" associated with the UFO/occult phenomena.

I have had many others who have contacted me about UFO experiences. Usually I have reservations, I know enough about the subject to be able to think of various explanations. Nevertheless, sometimes particular incidents are at least thought-provoking. There is often a remarkable similarity in the descriptions, a pattern indicating a purposeful agenda.

Here is one such incident.

A Large Illuminated Saucer

As I write this paragraph I have in my hand two 35 mm colored slides. Except for one feature, they are virtually identical. In the foreground is a mass of the sand of the desert in Arizona. In the middle of the picture is a raised mountainous area. Then rising above the mountain is the blue sky. The pictures were taken within seconds of each other.

The one feature that is different is that at the left of the second picture there is what looks like a large illuminated saucer at the side of the mountain, its light reflected down on to the mountain itself. What is so strange? Well, two things. First, the picture is hard to explain as just natural phenomena, or a technical fault in the film. It's for all the world like the typical "flying saucer"—reflected light and all—and it clearly is not there in the first picture. And, as we have said, those two pictures are separated only by seconds.

The second point? Probably just an interesting coincidence. The couple who took those slides were fine Christian people. Their names? Mr. and Mrs. Asher. As I say, probably just coincidence. But look back at those earlier chapters about "Mr. Asher." There is every reason to believe that occult powers test out some people to see if they have potential as contactees. Crazy isn't it, but is it just possible that the name "Asher" attracted special interest?

The Ashers are typical of people who have contacted me at meetings where I have spoken on this subject. I don't like talking about UFOs, and if the choice is left to me, I speak on other subjects such as the relevance of archaeology to the Bible. But when I do speak on the subject, sometimes I assure people I will not make them come to the front, or be embarrassed by being asked to tell their story publicly and then I ask: "How many here have seen a UFO?" It is not at all unusual to see a large number of hands raised. Sometimes I have asked them to write their experiences down briefly.

Quite often these writings are not convincing, and I have the distinct impression that the explanations for these experiences are quite mundane. But at other times they follow a pattern of consistency which highlights the reality of the UFO phenomenon. Usually they have not come forward earlier for fear of being ridiculed.

What The Alien Agenda Is

The fact is, UFOs are linked with aliens, spiritual entities, with clear-cut objectives. The Alien Agenda has been unchanged for centuries. This is not a pattern that has been designed only in the 1940's and updated for the 1980's. Their agenda is subject to change only because the agenda of their Opponent is not revealed in terms they fully understand.

The conflict is like a giant chessboard. There are skirmishes, maneuvers, checks, countermoves, but no possibility of a stalemate, or of a draw with the pieces to be set up again in friendly contest.

No. This is a fight to the death. But the aliens have lost their queen, their knights, their bishops. They hope, desperately hope against foolish hope that they can move their pawns forward to become proud queens again. The superior forces of the Opponent are clearly overwhelming but fight the aliens must. They have no hope of reprieve, no second game. And the Opponent is biding His time.

On The Nullarbor Plains In Australia

Another typical case is that of the "Mundrabilla Incident" on the Australian Nullarbor Plains in January, 1988. Mrs. Faye Knowles and her three adult sons are adamant that they were terrorized by a dazzling object, like a giant egg in an eggcup, that followed them as they maneuvered their car. It then landed on their roof, drew the car up from the road, shook it violently, and deposited it back on the road.

The Knowles' voices were altered, as though speaking at half rate on a tape recorder, deep voices that were quite different than normal. A strange dust was on their vehicle, there was a smell like that of dead bodies, and there were clear indentations on the roof of their car.

Truck drivers traversing the Nullarbor at the same time testified to seeing the strange light, and tuna fishermen in the Great Australian Bight to the south had reported similar phenomena some days previously.

Truck driver Graham Henley saw them 20 minutes

after the incident. The *Sun* (Melbourne, Australia, of January 25, 1988) commented:

"Mr. Henley said "shell shocked" members of the Knowles family received medical treatment for a 'nervous condition at the weekend.'
"He said theories aimed at debunking Wednesday's encounter near the [Western Australia-Southern Australia] border were 'a lot of rot.'
"One theory was that the dust on the car roof came from over-heated brakes.
" 'I felt the sooty material on the roof on the car, it was not brake dust,' Mr. Henley said. 'I've been around the car racing scene and I know what brake dust is like. This stuff was a fine silicon-type material. It was like powdered glass, it had an incredible feel to it. Brake dust only gets on the wheels, not on the roof and the brakes weren't even hot. It was the coolest part of the day and the road is virtually straight for about 75 km, so they would hardly have used their brakes.' "

The report goes on to state that Mr. Henley was convinced of the genuineness of the Knowles' experience:

"I knew they had seen something when I saw the terror on their faces—even the dog was cowering in the car. Mrs. Knowles was near hysterics. One of the boys is still in a state of shock. I have seen people after they've had bad accidents and the Knowles are even more shocked. These people were absolutely terrified. I am totally convinced that they had a terrifying experience but I can't explain it. Despite their hysteria everything was exactly as they described it when we went back to the scene."

He further says that they saw the footprints where the family went back to the bushes to hide, and they also saw the marks left by the U-turn as they drove to get away from the UFO.

The Knowles family had medical treatment during the weekend, apparently for a nervous disorder.

Mr. Henley discussed the way the Knowles family

had been ridiculed. He mentioned that there was no rain or lightning in the area and no street lights for miles. As for the marks on the roof supposedly left by the UFO, he elaborated:

"The Knowles' claimed dents in their car roof were caused by the UFO picking up their vehicle. There is no way that car was rolled because the front end was not misaligned, nor was there the damage you would get from rolling a car. One dent in the roof was particularly pronounced but I hit the roof and couldn't make a dent."

The report also tells of a statement by another "local," Mrs. Pajauta Patupis of Eucla near the state border. She claimed she had seen what appeared to be a UFO about nine p.m. on January 5. She further claimed that it was a craft with red and white flashing lights. Her husband saw it with her:

"My husband and I saw it coming from the west, it turned around and sort of stood still. It was very close to the ground. The strangest thing was that it had no engine noise. We reported it to air traffic control in Perth and they said there were no planes in the area."

There were, as usual, plenty of explanations to show that it was all just natural phenomena—a burst tire, dust from brake linings—and so on.

The *Courier* (Ballarat, Australia) of January 23, 1988, has Allan Brunt, former head of the South Australian Bureau of Meteorology putting forward the argument that it was an extremely distorted view of the setting sun.

Others suggested an electrical disturbance, a carbonaceous meteorite, or something "on the fringe of fairyland," but in the main the opinion was that the Knowles had indeed experienced something terrifying. A medical report pointed to such a conclusion.

One disturbing aspect, so far as this writer was concerned, was to see the way certain skeptics debunked the whole thing without having seen any member of the Knowles family, nor having examined their vehicle, nor having visited the area to see if there was any physical evidence at the site.

The attitude, "it must be nonsense," demonstrates a prejudgment that is not acceptable, whether there were natural phenomena involved or not. It is not a genuine investigation when the judge has given his verdict without examining the witnesses themselves or the available evidence.

Perhaps some of those critics have really had a field day. Or maybe we should say, "a sand day." For there's plenty of sand on the Nullarbor, sand for people with ostrich heads to hide in.

Whether the experience of the Knowles family really did involve the Aliens or not, the fact is that some critics rushed in to explain it all away, without talking to the victims, without examining their car, without studying on-the-spot reports, without comparing this case with so many others that have involved terror, trauma, tragedy.

In other areas of research such methodology would be rejected out of hand. The fact is, this is serious. The aliens *are* here. We say, not from other planets. Not from outer space. Not just from the innermost depths of human reality. We say the answer is paraphysical and that the author of terror is himself the perpetrator of these phenomena.

The Alien Agenda is being processed. Don't mock. Don't laugh. You or your spouse or your children might be the next victims.

Join those Christians who believe that the future is indeed bright. Join them as they look up to those same heavens where the UFOs are witnessed as false signs of the power of evil.

Join those Christians as they cry with the writer of the last Book of the Bible, the Revelation, "Even so, come Lord Jesus."

NOTES

Notes

In the main, the incidents referred to are documented, either in the body of the writing or in footnotes. Some incidents and theories appear widely in UFO writings and specific sources are not referred to.

CHAPTER 1

1. *Flying Saucers from Outer Space*, by Donald E. Keyhoe, p. 35.
2. One survey is *The New Guinea Episode* by Jacques Vallee, in *Flying Saucer Reader*, pp. 26-29.
3. *The Report on Unidentified Flying Objects* by Edward J. Ruppelt, published by Victor Gollancz, 1956.
4. *Flying Saucers Through the Ages* by Paul Thomas, p. 25.
5. Elaborated in *The Air Force Point of View* by Bill Wise in *Flying Saucer Reader*, pp. 189-191.
6. Quoted in *Flying Saucers—Myths, Madness, or Made in Moscow?* Don Boys, p. 12.
7. Summarized in *UFOs Plotted on a Map of France*, in *Flying Saucer Reader*, pp. 172-182.
8. *UFOs . . . Operation Trojan Horse*, by John A. Keel, p. 150.
9. *The Eternal Subject*, by Brinsley Le Poer Trench, pp. 170-182.
10. Keel, op. cit., p. 142.
11. Trench, op. cit., p. 25.
12. Ibid., pp. 24 ff.
13. *The Sun-Herald*, Sydney, Australia, January 23, 1966, pp. 3-4.
14. Elaborated in Chapter 12 of this volume.
15. See *Unsolved Mysteries of the Past*, by Otto Binder, p. 61.

CHAPTER 2

1. *The UFO Experience: A Scientific Inquiry*, by J. Allen Hynek, p. 144.
2. Quoted in *Flying Saucers from Outer Space*, by Donald E. Keyhoe, p. 35.
3. Ibid. (Frontispiece).
4. Keyhoe, op. cit., p. 34.
5. *Flying Saucers Through the Ages*, by Paul Thomas, p. 25.
6. Ibid., p. 41.
7. Ibid., pp. 249-252.
8. *Spacelink*, Vol. 6, No. 4, April, 1971, p. 20.
9. Keyhoe, op. cit., pp. 60-62.
10. Keel, op. cit., pp. 32-33.

11. Brad Steiger, *UFOs in the Deep Freeze*, in *Flying Saucer Reader*, p. 36.
12. Keel, op. cit., p. 16.
13. Ibid., p. 18.
14. Hynek, op. cit., p. 1.
15. Ibid., p. 2.

CHAPTER 3

1. Ibid., p. 86.
2. See e.g., Trench, op. cit., pp. 53-55.
3. *Gods, Demons and UFOs*, by Eric Norman, pp. 169-193.
4. Binder, op. cit., pp. 27 ff.

CHAPTER 4

1. *Spacelink*, Vol. 6, No. 4, April, 1971, back cover.
2. Keyhoe, op. cit., p. 48.
3. Ibid., p. 48.
4. Ibid., p. 52.
5. Ibid., p. 41.
6. *Australian Flying Saucer Review*, No. 7, November, 1962, pp. 1-2.
7. Binder, op. cit., p. 164.
8. For other examples, see Binder, ibid., pp. 163-165.
9. Flying Saucers—UFO Reports, No. 4, 1967, pp. 10 ff.
10. Binder, op. cit., pp. 164-165.
11. Keyhoe, op. cit., pp. 65-66.
12. *Flying Saucers are Hostile*, by Brad Steiger and Joan Whritenow, p. 81.
13. Binder, op. cit., p. 171.
14. *Radar News*, Vol. 11, No. 10, 1966, published in St. Petersburg, Florida, p. 1.

CHAPTER 5

1. Hynek, op. cit., p. 139.
2. Ibid., p. 139.
3. Keel, op. cit., p. 185.
4. Ibid., p. 282.
5. Ibid., p. 306.
6. Ibid., p. 274.
7. Ibid., pp. 30-31.
8. Binder, op. cit., p. 39.
9. Ibid., p. 40.
10. Ibid., p. 41.
11. Ibid., p. 48.
12. Trench, op. cit., Chapter 12.
13. Binder, op. cit., pp. 51-52.
14. Trench, op. cit., pp. 75ff.

CHAPTER 6

1. Binder, op. cit., pp. 43-44.
2. Ibid., pp. 44-45.

3. Ibid., pp. 55-56.
4. Ibid., pp. 38-39.
5. Keel, op. cit., pp. 156-157.
6. Keyhoe. op. cit., pp. 205 ff.
7. Hynek, op. cit., p. 141.
8. Keel, op. cit., p. 93.
9. Ibid., p. 131.
10. Ibid., p. 132.
11. Quoted in *Flying Saucers from Outer Space*, p. 57.
12. Keyhoe, op. cit., pp. 66-71.
13. Ibid., p. 70.
14. Details of the sightings are also given by Edward J. Ruppelt, *The Washington National Sightings*, in *The Flying Saucer Reader*, pp. 17-25.

CHAPTER 7

1. Binder, op. cit., p. 71.
2. Quoted in *UFOs ... Operation Trojan Horse*, p. 172.
3. See e.g., Binder, op. cit., pp. 70-71.
4. Ibid., p. 62.
5. Ibid., p. 60.
6. Ibid., p. 45.
7. Ibid., p. 42.
8. See e.g., Trench, op. cit., pp. 86 ff.
9. See e.g., Keel, op. cit., pp. 88 ff.
10. Ibid., p. 81.
11. Ibid., p. 297.
12. *Flying Blocks of Ice,* by Michael Harvey. (In *Canadian UFO Report*, Vol. 2, No. 4, 1971, pp. 25-26.)
13. Ibid., p. 25.
14. See e.g., Keel (op. cit.), pp. 165-166, 176, 183, 250, 298, and Binder (op. cit.), pp. 129-130.
15. Keel, op. cit., p. 139.
16. Binder, op. cit., p. 69.
17. Hynek, op. cit., p. 191.
18. Binder, op. cit., p. 69.
19. Ibid., p. 91.
20. Ibid., p. 104.
21. Published by the Australian Institute of Archaeology, 174 Collins Street, Melbourne, Australia.
22. *Spacelink*, Vol. 6, No. 3, June, 1970, p. 25.
23. *Crash Go the Chariots*, Clifford Wilson, p. 27 ff.
24. In *Flying Saucers: UFO Reports*, pp. 36 ff.
25. See e.g., Binder, op. cit., pp. 90, 94.
26. *Aku-Aku*, pp. 126 ff.
27. *Chariots of the Gods?* (Australian edition), by Erich Von Daniken, p. 72.
28. Ibid., pp. 12, 155.
29. Ibid., pp. 106-107.
30. *Crash Go the Chariots*, pp. 117-118.
31. c.f. *Chariots of the Gods?* p. 17, and *Crash Go the Chariots*, pp. 117-118.
32. Von Daniken, op. cit., pp. 31-32, cf. *Crash Go the Chariots*, pp. 12 ff.

33. *Crash Go the Chariots,* pp. 76-77.

CHAPTER 8

1. See e.g., Binder, op. cit., pp. 185-186, Keel, op. cit., pp. 220, 302. Also see *They Knew Too Much About Flying Saucers,* Gray Barker; and *Flying Saucers and the Three Men,* Albert K. Bender.
2. Keyhoe, op. cit., pp. 34-35.
3. Keel, op. cit., p. 82.
4. Ibid, p. 34.
5. Keyhoe, op. cit., p. 213.
6. *Spacelink,* Vol. 6, No. 2, January, 1970, p. 9.
7. Hynek, op. cit., p. 142.
8. Keel, op. cit., p. 213.
9. *Flying Saucers Over Australia,* compiled by Stephen Holledge, p. 119.
10. Keel, op. cit., p. 198.
11. Ibid., p. 275.
12. Ibid., pp. 213-214, 300.
13. Ibid., p. 278.
14. Ibid., p. 282.
15. Ibid., pp. 280 ff.

CHAPTER 9

1. The New Guinea sighting is reported in many journals and books. One interesting analysis is by Jacques Vallee, *The New Guinea Episode,* in *The Flying Saucer Reader,* pp. 26-29.
2. *Spacelink,* Vol. 6, No. 1, July, 1969, p. 4.
3. Ibid., Vol. 6, No. 2. January, 1970, pp. 21-22.
4. Hynek, op. cit., pp. 195 ff.
5. See elaboration at Keyhoe, op. cit., p. 76.
6. Ibid., p. 112.
7. Ibid., pp. 110-111.
8. Ibid., p. 92.
9. Hynek, op. cit., p. 241.
10. Ibid., p. 150.
11. Ibid., pp. 241-242.
12. Printed in *Flying Saucer Reader,* pp. 132-144.

CHAPTER 10

1. See e.g., *Is There a World Inside Our Planet?* by Raymond Bernard, in *Flying Saucer Reader,* pp. 101-107.
2. Keel, op. cit., p. 284.
3. Ibid., p. 284.
4. e.g., Steiger and Whritenow, op. cit., p. 123.
5. Ibid., pp 124-125.
6. *The Bible and Flying Saucers,* by Barry H. Downing, p. 148.
7. Ibid., p. 149.
8. Ibid., p. 150.
9. Keyhoe, op. cit., p. 42.
10. Ibid., p. 244.
11. Ibid., p. 245.

12. *Spacelink*, Vol. 5, No. 2, March, 1968, p. 26.
13. *They Knew Too Much About Flying Saucers*, by Gray Barker, p. 11.
14. Keel, op. cit., pp. 208 ff.
15. Binder, op. cit., p. 115.

CHAPTER 11

1. *The True Report on Flying Saucers*, by Donald E. Keyhoe, p. 29.
2. Ibid., p. 31.
3. Keyhoe, *Flying Saucers from Outer Space*, pp. 132-133.
4. Ibid., p. 135.
5. Ibid., p. 136.
6. Ibid., pp. 138-139.
7. Ibid., pp. 115-116.
8. Ibid., p. 100.
9. Ibid., p. 150.
10. Ibid., p. 66.
11. Ibid., pp. 113 ff.
12. Keel, op. cit., p. 28.
13. Ibid., pp. 55-56.
14. Ibid., p. 57.
15. Ibid., p. 57.
16. In *The New York Times* of August 23, 1966, Evert Clark discusses this theory and related topics put forward by Philip Klass, electronics editor of *Aviation Week and Space Technology*.
17. Keel, op. cit., p. 63.
18. Hynek, op. cit., pp. 226-227.
19. Keyhoe, op. cit., pp. 131-146, 211-215, and especially pp. 143-144.

CHAPTER 12

1. *The UFO Experience: A Scientific Inquiry*, by J. Allen Hynek.
2. Keyhoe, op. cit., p. 89.
3. See W. Gordon Allen, *UFOs and the Sonic Boom*, in *Flying Saucer Reader*, pp. 45-49.
4. Quoted by Keel, op. cit., p. 39.
5. Ibid., pp. 39 ff.
6. Ibid., p. 42.
7. Ibid., p. 44.
8. Ibid., p. 182.
9. Ibid., p. 58.
10. Ibid., p. 59.
11. Ibid., p. 59.
12. Ibid., p. 60.
13. Trench, op. cit., p. 83.
14. Ibid., p. 58.
15. Ibid., pp. 51-53.
16. Steiger and Whritenow, op. cit., p. 58 ff.
17. Keel, op. cit., p. 44.
18. Ibid., p. 44.
19. Ibid., p. 45.

20. Ibid., pp. 46-47.
21. Ibid., p. 47.
22. Ibid., p. 36.
23. Hynek, op. cit., p. 229.
24. Ibid., p. 232.

CHAPTER 13

1. Keel, op. cit., p. 219.
2. Ibid., p. 233.
3. Binder, op. cit., p. 172.
4. Keel, op. cit., p. 213.
5. Ibid., p. 290.
6. Ibid., p. 205.
7. Ibid., pp. 66-68.
8. Ibid., p. 67.
9. Ibid., pp. 185 ff.
10. Ibid., p. 183.
11. Ibid., p. 199.
12. Ibid., p. 199.
13. Ibid., p. 199.
14. Binder, op. cit., pp. 39-40.
15. Keel, op. cit., p. 234.
16. Ibid., p. 248.
17. Ibid., p. 237.
18. Ibid., p. 243.
19. Ibid., pp. 256-270.
20. Ibid., p. 270.
21. Ibid., p. 271.
22. Ibid., p. 215.
23. Ibid., p. 217.

CHAPTER 14

1. *Crash Go the Chariots*, p. 121.
2. Binder, op. cit., p. 121.
3. Ibid., p. 121.
4. Keil and Delitzsch, *Commentary on the Old Testament*, Vol. 1, p. 131.
5. Ibid., Vol. III, p. 290.
6. Ibid., Vol. III, p. 294.
7. *The Bible and Flying Saucers*, by Barry H. Downing, p. 105.
8. *Chariots of the Gods?* p. 57.
9. Downing, op. cit., p. 134.

Life International. Time-Life International (Nederland), Amsterdam, Netherlands. April 18, 1966. Vol. 40, No. 8.

Men in the Flying Saucers Identified. W. V. Grant.

Radar News. Cathedral Caravan, Inc. Vol. 11, No. 4.

Radar News. Cathedral Caravan, Inc. Vol. 11, No. 10.

Saga's UFO Special. Gambi Publications, Inc., New York, Vol. III.

Scientific American. October, 1973. Vol. 229, No. 4.

Spacelink. March, 1968. Volume 5, No. 2.

Spacelink. July, 1969. Volume 6, No. 1.

Spacelink. January, 1970. Volume 6, No. 2.

Spacelink. June, 1970. Volume 6, No. 3.

Spacelink. April, 1971. Volume 6, No. 4.

The True Report on Flying Saucers. Fawcett Publications, Inc., Greenwich, Conn. No. 1.

Holledge, James. *Flying Saucers Over Australia.* Horwitz Publications Inc. Pty. Ltd., Australia, 1965.

Hynek, J. Allen. *The UFO Experience: A Scientific Inquiry.* Abelard-Schuman Ltd., New York, 1972.

Jessup, M. K. *The Expanding Case for UFO.* Arco Publications Ltd., London, 1957.

Keel, John A. *UFOs ... Operation Trojan Horse.* Sphere Books Ltd., London, 1973

Keil, C. F., and Delitzsch, F. *Commentary on the Old Testament.* William B. Eerdmans Publishing Company, Grand Rapids, Michigan.

Keyhoe, Donald E. *Flying Saucers from Outer Space.* Univeral-Tandem Publishing Co. Ltd., 1970.

Kitchen, K. A. *Ancient Orient and Old Testament.* The Tyndale Press, London, 1966.

Lindsay, Gordon. *The Antichrists Have Come.* The Voice of Healing Publishing Company, Dallas, Texas, 1958.

Lorenzen, Coral and Jim. *Flying Saucer Occupants.* A Signet Book published by the New American Library, Inc., New York, 1967.

Michel, Aimé. *The Truth About Flying Saucers.* Robert Hale Ltd., London, 1957.

Norkin, Israel. *Saucer Diary.* Pageant Press, Inc., New York, 1957.

Norman, Eric. *Gods, Demons, and UFOs.* Lancer Books, Inc., New York, 1970.

Ruppelt, Edward J., *The Report on Unidentified Flying Objects,* Victor Gollancz, 1956.

Sendy, Jean, *The Coming of the Gods.* Berkley Publishing Corporation, New York, 1970.

Steiger, Brad, and Whritenow, Joan. *Flying Saucers Are Hostile.* Universal Publishing and Distributing Corporation, New York, 1967.

Steiger, Brad, and Whritenow, Joan. *Allende Letters.* Univeral-Tandem Publishing Co. Ltd., London, 1968.

Tambling, Richard. *Flying Saucers: Where Do They Come From?* Horwitz Publications Inc. Pty. Ltd., Australia, 1967.

Thomas, Paul. *Flying Saucers Through the Ages.* Neville Spearman Ltd., London, 1965.

Trench, Brinsley Le Poer. *The Eternal Subject.* Souvenir Press Ltd., London, 1973.

Von Daniken, Erich. *Chariots of the Gods?* Bantam Books, Inc., New York, 1973.

Wilson, Clifford. *Crash Go the Chariots.* Lancer Books Inc., New York, 1972.

Wilson, Clifford. *In the Beginning God.* Word of Truth Productions Ltd., Victoria, Australia, 1970.

JOURNALS AND OCCASIONAL PAPERS HAVE INCLUDED

Australian Flying Saucer Review. November, 1962. No. 7.

Canadian UFO Report. J. F. Magor, 1971. Vol. 2, No. 4 (Whole No. 12).

Flying Saucers, UFO Reports. Dell Publishing Co., Inc., New York, No. 4.

Everybody's. January 11, 1967.

Bibliography

Not all the books here listed are of the same quality. They are included because they have been available to the author in the preparation of this volume. Those from which quotations have been made are as listed for each chapter.

In this investigation three books have been of special value. They are:

Flyin Saucers from Outer Space, by Donald E. Keyhoe, giving much relevant information in the early days of modern UFO sightings;

UFOs ... Operation Trojan Horse, by John A. Keel, whose research and startling conclusions bring the subject into the 1970s; and

The UFO Experience: A Scientific Inquiry, by J. Allen Hynek. This has been of special value because it came from a highly qualified U.S. consultant who became disillusioned with some of the "official" explanations.

Adamski, George, *Flying Saucers Farewell*. Abelard-Schuman Ltd., New York, 1961.

Barker, Gray. *They Knew Too Much About Flying Saucers*. T. Werner Laurie Ltd., London, 1958.

Bender, Albert K. *Flying Saucers and the Three Men*. Neville Spearman Ltd., London, 1963.

Binder, Otto. *Unsolved Mysteries of the Past*. Tower Publications, Inc., New York.

Binder, Otto. *What We Really Know About Flying Saucers*. Fawcett Publications, Inc., 1967.

Boys, Don. *Flying Saucers: Myths, Madness, or Made in Moscow?* Goodhope Press, Indianapolis, Ind.

Condon, Edward U., Extracts from *Scientific Study of Unidentified Flying Objects*. Ed. Daniel S. Gilmer, Bantam Books, N.Y., 1969.

Cove, Gordon. *Who Pilots the Flying Saucers?* Evangel Press, London.

David, Jay. *The Flying Saucer Reader*. The New American Library, Inc., New York, 1967.

Downing, Barry H. *The Bible and Flying Saucers*. Avon Books, New York, 1970.

Green, Gabriel. *Let's Face the Facts About Flying Saucers*. Popular Library, New York, 1967.

Greenfield, Irving A. *The UFO Report*. Lancer Books, Inc., New York, 1967.

Heard, Gerald. *Is Another World Watching?* Bantam Books, New York, 1953.

BIBLIOGRAPHY